UNITED WE STAND

UNITED WE STAND

A History of Oneness Organizations

Arthur L. Clanton

THE PENTECOSTAL PUBLISHING HOUSE
8855 DUNN ROAD
HAZELWOOD, MISSOURI
1970

ISBN 0-912315-42-3

Copyright 1970 by
Pentecostal Publishing House
All Rights Reserved

No part of this book may be reproduced by any means, including mimeographing, photocopying, or recording, without the written permission of the publisher.

FOREWORD

In reading the manuscript for *United We Stand,* I was deeply impressed by the vast store of pertinent information it contained. I was made to realize that extensive research had gone into its writing.

Undoubtedly, this book will be sincerely appreciated by our people, as it gives a complete history of the Oneness organizations, in addition to telling how God revealed the truth of Oneness and baptism in Jesus' name.

This history of the Oneness organizations which preceded, and led to the formation of, the United Pentecostal Church, makes an interesting story indeed. The account should make us all thankful for the way God led His people on in the glorious gospel truth.

I have no hesitancy in recommending *United We Stand* to our people, and to anyone else interested in Oneness history.

My sincere congratulations go to the author for a job well-done.

PAUL H. BOX

AUTHOR'S PREFACE

The author of *United We Stand* was appointed editor of United Pentecostal Church publications in 1955.

When he came into office, he was delighted to find on file old copies of the official organs of the two largest Oneness Pentecostal organizations prior to the 1945 merger: The Pentecostal Church, Incorporated and the Pentecostal Assemblies of Jesus Christ. There was the Apostolic Herald, official voice of the Pentecostal Ministerial Alliance from January, 1926 until October, 1932, and then of the Pentecostal Church, Incorporated until 1945. Then there was the Pentecostal Outlook, official voice of the Pentecostal Assemblies of Jesus Christ from January, 1932 until 1945.

Later, Assistant General Superintendent Oliver F. Fauss brought into the office of the editor copies of an even older periodical—the Pentecostal Witness, dating from November, 1924 until November, 1931. This publication was, first, the official voice of the Texas District of the Pentecostal Assemblies of the World. Following this, it served the same purpose in Emmanuel's Church in Jesus Christ, and, still later, in the Apostolic Church of Jesus Christ.

Of course, from the time of the merger of the Pentecostal Assemblies of Jesus Christ and the Pentecostal Church, Incorporated in 1945, there was the Pentecostal Herald, official voice of the United Pentecostal Church.

Thus, there were available continuous publications of Oneness Pentecostal organizations from 1924.

The editor avidly read these periodicals, keenly enjoying the history they revealed. He realized that relatively few persons then living had been privileged to read many of these interesting happenings.

This realization gave birth to the idea of writing such a book as *United We Stand*. It was felt that the historical events contained in the aforementioned periodicals should be shared with all who were interested.

More than three years of tiring work have gone into the writing of this book. Every issue of the different periodicals was carefully read, and voluminous notes taken. In addition, minutes of board meetings and conferences, along with old manuals, were examined in detail, and relevant material taken from them. Then all the material was painstakingly organized, typed, and re-typed—some parts several times.

Other material sources deserve mention. The late Samuel C. McClain furnished many hand-written pages of notes, which proved invaluable. There was also vital word-of-mouth information from different ministers. All this is deeply appreciated.

It seems improbable that much could be added to the history of those earlier organizations mentioned in this work, since there are few, if any, written records available, other than those used herein. Further, most of the Pentecostal pioneers who lived these experiences have passed on to their reward.

In contradistinction, the history of the United Pentecostal Church is still being "written." Because of this, the chapter dealing with that organization will have to be revised and brought up-to-date as time passes. Other "Profiles" will also be added.

May God make the future history of this great organization even more glorious than that of the past.

INTRODUCTION

In setting forth what this book is, it seems best to first tell what it *is not*. This should eliminate any confusion concerning its purpose.

The book is not a general history of latter-day Pentecost. Such a work hardly seems necessary, as others have already covered this ground. It is true that some still among us were saved in Trinitarian churches, and Oneness does, therefore, have its roots in early-day Pentecost. But several other books tell of happenings during the first few years after the latter-day outpouring of the Holy Ghost.

Secondly, the book does not primarily concern itself with biographical sketches of well-known Pentecostal ministers. One chapter, *Profiles in Pentecost,* does contain short biographies of Oneness ministers. But these profiles are of only those ministers mentioned elsewhere in the book, and are included to make it more interesting and inspirational.

Lastly, this is not a history of the Oneness movement in general. Happenings among Oneness Pentecostal people before any Oneness organization was formed are mentioned only to lay groundwork for, and to show the necessity of, their organizing.

This book is, then, primarily a history of Oneness *organizations*. It tells how and why these organizations were established. It goes into detail concerning the inner workings of these organizations. Especially is this true of chapter eleven: The United Pentecostal Church.

The purpose of the book is threefold: (1) to provide a detailed history of Oneness organizations for present and future generations; (2) to furnish a text for those who are called upon to make an in-depth study of Oneness Pentecostal organizations; and (3) to place in the hands of those "outside" an authentic account of the history, doctrine and polity of Oneness organizations, particularly of the United Pentecostal Church.

It is the prayer of the author that this book will bring about a deeper appreciation for our Oneness heritage.

ARTHUR L. CLANTON

CONTENTS

1. Pre-Organization Oneness	13
2. The General Assembly of the Apostolic Assemblies	23
3. The Pentecostal Assemblies of the World	27
4. The Pentecostal Ministerial Alliance	35
5. Emmanuel's Church in Jesus Christ	52
6. The Apostolic Church of Jesus Christ	62
7. The Pentecostal Assemblies of Jesus Christ	70
8. The Pentecostal Church, Incorporated	87
9. Unsuccessful Attempts at Merger	105
10. The Merger	116
11. The United Pentecostal Church	128
12. Profiles in Pentecost	183
Epilogue: The Backward and Forward Look	202

1
Pre-Organization Oneness

One who makes a careful study of the *Oneness* * movement soon comes upon a truth not generally known: Some converts were baptized in Jesus' name from nearly as far back as 1901, when the latter-day outpouring of the Holy Ghost began.

In 1902, Charles F. Parham wrote a book entitled *A Voice Crying in the Wilderness,* in which he said, "Then how quickly we recognized the fact that we could not be buried by baptism in the name of the Father, and in the name of the Holy Ghost, because it stood for nothing, as they never died, and were never resurrected. So if you desire to witness a public confession of a clean conscience toward God and man, and faith in the divinity of Jesus Christ, you will be baptized by single immersion, signifying the death, burial, and resurrection; being baptized in the name of Jesus, into the name of the Father, Son, and Holy Ghost; they are one when in Christ you become one with all." [1]

Howard A. Goss was baptized in Jesus' name in 1903. This is confirmed by S. C. McClain, who wrote, "In the year of 1903, the revival had swept into many cities and villages, and in Galena, Kansas, H. A. Goss was converted, and buried in Jesus' name through water baptism." [2] In 1915, Goss was

---

* For a definition of Oneness, see page 142.
[1] Foster, Think It Not Strange, p. 70.
[2] Ibid., p. 71.

again baptized in Jesus' name, because he had not fully realized the significance of his earlier baptism.[3]

Other church historians confirm that some had used the shorter baptismal formula since shortly after 1900, and that many others who did not use it, still thought it acceptable. The shorter formula was, of course, "in the name of the Lord Jesus Christ," instead of "in the name of the Father, and of the Son, and of the Holy Ghost."

There is nothing strange in their baptizing in Jesus' name. Honest Bible students, reading the Book of Acts to learn of the baptism of the Holy Ghost, would come naturally upon the truth of water baptism in Jesus' name. There is no mystery connected with this truth. It is simply a matter of doing what the Bible plainly teaches.

The manner in which Bible study led many into the truth of baptism in Jesus' name is illustrated by the experience of Andrew D. Urshan. In the year of 1910, while praying and meditating, he heard a voice within him, saying, "The Father, the Son, the Holy Ghost; the Lord Jesus Christ." He immediately began to study the Book of Acts anew. Said he, "As I looked up the scriptures over and over, a serious question was created within me: Why did the apostles baptize Jews, Samaritans, and Gentiles in the name of Jesus Christ. . . ? One day, while searching the Scriptures, the Lord called my attention to two words in Matthew 28:19 — THE NAME. I then began to baptize new converts into the name of the Lord Jesus Christ."[4] Remember, this happened in 1910!

The question arises, "Why did not **every** Holy Ghost-filled minister baptize in the name of Jesus?" It seems likely that, as more and more ministers of other denominations came into Pentecost, they, not giving themselves to Bible study as had earlier ministers, simply continued using the old denominational formula.

---

[3] Ibid.
[4] Witness of God, November, 1962, pp. 2, 3.

It was not until 1913, however, that the truth of the Oneness of the Godhead was fully revealed; and, along with it, the doctrine of water baptism in Jesus' name was thrust out into the open.

Frank J. Ewart wrote: "At the great world-wide camp meeting held in Arroyo Seco, California in 1913, there were hundreds of preachers present from all over the nation and Canada . . .

"One day a preacher spoke from the passage in Jeremiah 31:22. The very suggestion of God's doing a new thing struck fire in the minds and hearts of the saints, and from then on to the end of the camp, one could hear expressions of hope that God would soon do a new thing for His people. The new thing was exhibited to those who had ears and eyes to perceive it.

"The occasion was a baptismal service in the pool near the big tent. Brother Scott had selected Evangelist R. E. McAlister to preach on the subject of water baptism . . . He concluded his sermon abruptly by saying, 'The apostles invariably baptized their converts once in the name of Jesus Christ; that the words Father, Son, and Holy Ghost were never used in Christian baptism.'" [5]

In this camp meeting there was a man by the name of John G. Scheppe, who spent an entire night in prayer. During the night, God revealed to him the truth of Oneness and baptism in Jesus' name. He ran through the camp, shouting to all what the Lord had shown him. This led many others to search the Scriptures, and the result was that they, too, saw that baptism must be administered in the name of the Lord Jesus Christ.

Sitting in the congregation at this camp meeting were three who were to become staunch advocates for Oneness and baptism in Jesus' name. The three were Frank J. Ewart, G. T. Haywood, and Harry Morse. Of this occasion, Morse

---

[5] Ewart, The Phenomenon of Pentecost, p. 76.

wrote, "After we listened to Brother Scheppe's new ideas on water baptism in Jesus' name, and the oneness of the Godhead, we agreed that we believed that he had something. We finally left one another from the camp meeting. In the following months, God began to deal with Brother Ewart, Brother Haywood, and finally with me, and we came out on this line...." [6]

Speaking of the time in late 1913 or early 1914, Ewart said, "For months God had been dealing with me about the name of God, and its place in the gospel preached by the apostles. At last I decided to obey God, and step out with His message, which, by this time, was clearly defined in my soul.

"I preached my first sermon on Acts 2:38 on April 15, 1914. The message took fire, and that night a revival started. Brother Glenn A. Cook had come back from an eastern trip, and came out to the meeting that night. He accepted the message, and became my assistant in the tent campaign. We purchased a baptismal tank, and set it up inside the tent. I baptized Brother Cook, and he baptized me. Then the candidates for baptism in the name of Jesus started to flock to the tent." [7]

In January, 1915, Cook made another eastern evangelistic tour. He conducted services for one week in Mother Barnes' Faith Home in St. Louis. She and her entire staff were baptized in Jesus' name.

From St. Louis, Cook went to Indianapolis, the home of G. T. Haywood. This noted preacher was warned that Cook was coming with an erroneous doctrine. He replied, "The warning came too late. I have already been rebaptized."

Haywood's baptism led many more to accept the truth. Ewart confirms this by saying, ". . . In Indianapolis, 475 were soon baptized into the name of Jesus, and most of these had

[6] Apostolic Herald, December, 1943, p. 9.
[7] Ewart, Phenomenon of Pentecost, p. 51.

Glenn Cook of Los Angeles, California baptizes L. V. Roberts of Indianapolis, Indiana, March 6, 1915, in the first Jesus' name baptismal service east of the Mississippi River.

already received the Holy Ghost baptism, or received it soon after being baptized." [8]

Ewart adds: "Elder G. T. Haywood . . . was mightily used of God until his untimely death (April 12, 1931, at the age of only 51), in proclaiming the name and absolute deity of our Lord Jesus Christ. Through his wonderful expositions, the colored people everywhere responded, and very few are left in the old ranks now." [9]

Andrew D. Urshan, mentioned earlier in this chapter, returned in 1916 from a two-year evangelistic tour in Persia and other countries. When he saw the disunited condition of the Pentecostal movement, he was deeply saddened, and decided to use his influence to bring the two factions back into unity. But after two years of hard work and fruitless effort, he gave up. Throughout the years, he stood for the absolute deity of Jesus, and for baptism in His name.[10] (He died October 16, 1967.)

Many other prominent ministers obeyed the truth, and were baptized in Jesus' name. Among those not already mentioned were E. N. Bell, L. C. Hall, W. E. Booth-Clibborn, R. J. Scott, A. H. Argue, Frank Small, George T. Studd, Elmer K. Fisher, W. T. Witherspoon, D. C. O. Opperman, H. C. Rodgers, Harry Van Loon, H. E. White, Robert L. LaFleur, Oliver F. Fauss, Harvey Shearer, and others. In addition, many laymembers were baptized, or re-baptized, in Jesus' name.

Among the ministers mentioned in the preceding paragraph, the case of E. N. Bell deserves special attention here, due to the strange turn it took. Bell was the first General Chairman of the Assemblies of God. However, at the time when the following events occurred, he had been replaced by A. P. Collins. He was still editor of the Weekly Evangel and the Word and Witness.

[8] Ibid., p. 53.
[9] Ibid., p. 56.
[10] Ibid., p. 78.

From March until July of 1915, Bell wrote articles in opposition to re-baptism in Jesus' name. But he had a quick change of heart and mind. In July, when he wrote his last article defending Trinitarian baptism, he himself was baptized in Jesus' name. The event occurred in the third Interstate Encampment of the Assemblies of God in Jackson, Tennessee. H. G. Rodgers was the camp pastor. The evangelist was L. V. Roberts, who had been baptized in Jesus' name by Glenn Cook in Indianapolis, on March 6, 1915. At the close of Roberts' first sermon, Bell and Rodgers were baptized in Jesus' name.

Bell now began to write in defense of the truth which he had recently opposed. In the August 14, 1915 Weekly Evangel he wrote an article entitled, "Who Is Jesus Christ?" Before the article was printed, copies of it were sent to all the General Presbyters. D. C. O. Opperman, one of these presbyters, received a copy. Later, he wrote, "Some of the presbyters objected to the last part of the article, which dealt with the Father's name being given to Jesus, and with baptism in Jesus' name, therefore that was cut out (before the article was printed), along with the mention of the fact that Bell had been baptized in Jesus' name. They did not want the people to know that he had been baptized in Jesus' name, and was teaching it." [11]

Limited space prevents reproduction of Bell's complete article here. But it is printed in its entirety, exactly as originally written, In Fauss' *Buy the Truth and Sell It Not*. A portion of the article follows:

"I want to thank God for the discussion of water baptism in the name of Jesus Christ, because it has proved the means of discovering to me a mightier Christ than I ever realized before. The water baptism issue in the name of Christ, taken alone, would be comparatively a small and tame matter. Just

---

[11] Opperman, The Blessed Truth, October 1, 1919.

so it at first seemed to me and to many others, and to some still, because they have not seen what is involved in it, and do not have the full apostolic vision of Jesus Christ as Lord or Jehovah . . .

"I can say today, before God and all men, that His joy is rolling in my soul now as never before. As I write, His glory convulses my whole physical frame, and I have to stop now and then and say, 'Glory,' or 'Oh glory,' and let some of it escape. Night before last, as I lay on my bed, I heard in the Spirit the sweetest, most soul-thrilling song on the wonderful name of Jesus I ever heard since I was born. If people knew what God is putting in my soul by a brand new vision of Jesus, and the wonders hid in His mighty and glorious name, they would cease pitying me for being baptized in the name of the Lord Jesus Christ, and begin to shout and help me praise the Lamb that was slain, who is now beginning to receive some honor and praise, but who will eventually make the whole universe — sea, earth and sky, reverberate with universal praise and honor to His great name. Hallelujah to His name forever and forever!

"I can now say in all sincerity that I do not believe Christ ever meant to baptize with the phrase 'Father and Son' at all. We have used it that way so long, at first it seemed to me absurd that we should do anything else. But now that I have received the real vision of Christ as the Lord, that Lord is the Father's name, and also the name of Christ, I wonder why I was ever so blind as not to see Christ's meaning in Matthew 28:19. All may baptize with the phrase in Matthew 28:19 who feel so led, and I will love and fellowship them just the same, but personally, with my present light, I could not conscientiously do so any more. I prefer to use the real name common to both Father and Son, as the Lord commanded me to baptize in the 'name,' not in a relationship phrase which is no proper name at all. Lord help the dear brethren to see that Father and Son are by no means proper names. . . ."

Reaction to Bell's baptism was varied. It seems apparent,

from his own words, that some pitied him. Ewart says, "Brother Bell met with a withering storm of opposition from his brethren, but he stood his ground (for a time), and defended his new position so unanswerably that many, many people were in doubt as to where this would lead. . . ." [12]

Trinitarian ministers in the Assemblies of God felt that Bell would, in time, reaffirm his belief in the Trinity. And this is exactly what he did. It seems little short of amazing that he could have been given such a revelation, as described by his own words, and then return to Trinitarian error.

Afterward, he again wrote against the truth of Oneness and baptism in Jesus' name. As late as 1919, he wrote an anti-Oneness article, entitled, *The Great Battle for the Truth.* D. C. O. Opperman, in his paper *The Blessed Truth,* answered Bell in an article headed, *Brother Bell is on Both Sides of the Fence.* Opperman said, "As we read his attack on the truth, our mind at once reverted to the article he wrote in the Weekly Evangel soon after he was baptized in Jesus' name. We thought it would be well to just let Brother Bell answer his own argument. Perhaps it may help him to recall the glory that flooded his soul when he walked with God in the light of the truth." [13] Opperman then reproduced Bell's article exactly as it had been originally written.

As previously mentioned, many Pentecostal ministers and laymen were being converted to the truth, and were being baptized in Jesus' name. Officials of the Assemblies of God felt that something must be done. Consequently, a General Council meeting was called in St. Louis during October, 1915. There, a mild statement was passed, more or less leaving the baptismal formula up to the individual, so long as he did not tear up assemblies, etc.

But a feeling of opposition was rising in the hearts of Trinitarian ministers. They wanted the issue of the Godhead

---

[12] The Phenomenon of Pentecost, p. 55.
[13] The Blessed Truth, October 1, 1919.

and water baptism settled once and for all. Consequently, it was announced that the Fourth General Council, to be held in St. Louis in October, 1916, would be an Open Bible Council.

At the Council, a committee was appointed to prepare a statement of fundamental beliefs for the organization. This statement was considered, and voted upon, point by point. Oneness members of the Assemblies of God voted solidly in opposition, but to no avail. The statement of beliefs was adopted, and this, in effect, forced the Oneness adherents out of the organization. The ministerial membership dropped from 585 to 429. Numerous assemblies were also forced out of fellowship with the organization.

In his book, *Buy the Truth, and Sell It Not,* O. F. Fauss spoke of the 1916 General Council in these words: "I was told that the Oneness brethren retired to the lobby of the meeting hall, and began to study what they should do. 'Where shall we go from here?' they asked."

This was a pertinent question. Certain conditions had earlier made it imperative that Pentecostal people organize, hence there had been brought into being the Assemblies of God. Those conditions still existed. Therefore, since Oneness ministers and churches had been forced out of the Assemblies of God, they must now form an organization of their own.

S. C. McClain put it this way: "After fellowship was completely broken between the Assemblies of God and those who baptized in Jesus' name, there seemed no other way out but to form a Oneness organization." [14]

---

[14] McClain, Unpublished Notes.

2
The General Assembly of the Apostolic Assemblies

Two months after they were forced out of the Assemblies of God (chapter one), the Oneness ministers took steps to form a new organization. A large group of ministers met in Eureka Springs, Arkansas on December 28, 1916. No business was transacted, however, until 2:30 p. m. on January 2, 1917. Another business meeting was held on January 3.

According to the minutes of the conference, the first order of business was the election of officers. D. C. O. Opperman was elected Chairman; Lee Floyd, Secretary; and Howard A. Goss, Treasurer. The term of office was one year.

It was then moved that the new organization be known as The General Assembly of the Apostolic Assemblies.

Howard A. Goss and H. G. Rodgers were appointed to serve with Opperman as a Credential Committee. The function of this committee was to prepare a form of credential for the new organization. The founding fathers saw no need to include a copy of this credential in their minutes. Said they, "It is unnecessary to specify the form of credentials . . . They are a simple form in which nothing of a doctrinal nature is embodied."

NOTE: The author is indebted to John Mark Opperman, son of the well-known Pentecostal pioneer, D. C. O. Opperman, for a copy of the Minute Book and Ministerial Record of the General Assembly of the Apostolic Assemblies. Most of the information in this chapter is taken from that book.

Each minister was asked to pay twenty-five cents annually for his credential.

Eighteen Articles of Faith were adopted by the General Assembly of the Apostolic Assemblies.

Article One concerned membership in the church. It read: "As members of the body of Christ, which is the true church (Ephesians 1:22, 23), the Word of God declares but one way of entrance therein, and that is 'By one Spirit are we all baptized into one body,' and that is a baptism of water and Spirit."

Article Four was entitled God's Standard of Salvation. It stated: "We earnestly contend for God's standard of salvation. In the Word of God we can find nothing short of a holy, Spirit-filled life, with signs following as on the Day of Pentecost."

Article Five pertained to Repentance and Remission of Sins. It read, in part: "John preached repentance. Jesus proclaimed it, and before His ascension commanded that repentance and remission of sins should be preached in His name, beginning at Jerusalem. And Peter fulfilled this command on the Day of Pentecost."

Other articles concerned divine healing, the Lord's Supper, the second coming of Jesus, the translation of the saints, the Millennium, the final judgment, and the living of a wholly sanctified life.

Strange as it may seem, no direct mention was made of baptism in the name of Jesus, or of the Oneness of the Godhead. Certainly every minister in the new organization believed in and preached these two cardinal doctrines. It was this belief and practice that had caused their expulsion from the Assemblies of God. But these Pentecostal pioneers were wary of binding one another's ministry. They felt that each should be given leeway to preach what was in his heart. They would have been content to have remained in the Assemblies of God, had this privilege not been denied them.

The first and only published ministerial list of the General Assembly of the Apostolic Assemblies contained 154 names. Not all these names can be mentioned here, but many of the ministers were prominent in Oneness Pentecostal circles. Among them were J. C. Brickey, W. E. Booth-Clibborn, Clarence Craine, John Die, E. J. Douglas, F. J. Ewart, O. F. Fauss, Lee Floyd, H. A. Goss, L. C. Hall, B. H. Hite, Robert LaFleur, S. C. McClain, D. K. Morris, Ben Pemberton, John Scheppe, W. L. Stallones, and S. L. Wise. (In inserting these names, the author had to depend upon his own personal knowledge as to who should be mentioned. Please forgive the omission of any name that should have been included.) Most of these ministers have gone on to their eternal reward.

At the time of the formation of the new organization, Daniel C. O. Opperman had been publishing *The Blessed Truth* in Eureka Springs for approximately two years. The General Assembly of the Apostolic Assemblies voted to make this periodical its official organ, and for Opperman to continue to serve as editor.

In common with all other Oneness organizations, this newly-formed one was missionary minded. The ministers voted that all missionary money be sent to Opperman, who would forward it to the missionaries. The ministerial list showed the names of seven missionaries.

Soon after the formation of the General Assembly of the Apostolic Assemblies, its ministers encountered a serious problem. America had entered the First World War on April 6, 1917. Since the organization had been in existence for such a short time, it could not get its young ministers exempt from military service.[1]

Another near essentiality in those days was the special clergy rate granted ministers by the railroads. Few ministers had automobiles, so most of them traveled by train. Apparently, the Clergy Bureau refused to recognize the newly-formed organization, and this worked a hardship on its ministers.

---

[1] McClain, Unpublished Notes

For these two reasons, the organization was destined to be short-lived. Perhaps it set a record at lasting for the shortest length of time of any organization, since it continued only until the end of the year. It had no conferences other than the one in which it was organized.

The plight of the young preachers was desperate; something had to be done for their protection. This led to the first Oneness merger.

3
The Pentecostal Assemblies of the World

The founding of this organization is shrouded in almost total obscurity. S. C. McClain states that it was formed by a minister named Frazier, late in 1914, in Portland, Oregon.[1] Morris E. Golder, Pentecostal Assemblies of the World minister, says that the minister's name was Frazee, and that the organization had its beginning in Los Angeles in 1915.[2]

By 1917, this group had been organized long enough to secure non-combatant status for its young ministers. For this reason, it seemed good to the Oneness ministers of the General Assembly of the Apostolic Assemblies to seek consolidation with the Pentecostal Assemblies of the World.

It is difficult to ascertain the exact date of this merger. S. C. McClain puts it in 1917 (apparently late), while O. F. Fauss states that it was in 1918 (apparently early). The two groups formed a new charter, and took the name of the older organization—the Pentecostal Assemblies of the World, adding the word "Incorporated."

This was an interracial organization. E. W. Doak, a white man, was elected General Chairman. G. T. Haywood, already mentioned in this work as a prominent Negro minister, was

---

[1] Foster, Think It Not Strange, p. 73.
[2] Telephone Conversation, September, 1969.

elected General Secretary. Daniel C. O. Opperman was chosen as General Elder.

In the first General Conference of the newly-merged group, held in Eureka Springs, Arkansas in 1918, few if any Negro ministers were present, and very little business was transacted.[3]

Intimate association with the Negro race was something new for the white ministers of the South. Says McClain, "I was from the South, where it had been considered improper for a white person to have equal fellowship with, or sit at a table with, Colored people. My wife, who had been raised in Indianapolis, thought nothing of these things.

"I asked her, 'Do we shake hands with Colored people?'

"Her answer was, 'Most certainly we do!'

"After I got used to it, I thought it was wonderful. I thought nothing of the color line." [4]

Certainly this attitude of McClain's was shared by many other Southern Oneness ministers. And later, when the white ministers left the Pentecostal Assemblies of the World, it was not because of racial prejudice on their part.

To fully understand the problems facing an interracial organization in the South then, one must understand something of the segregation laws, and rules based upon many years of tradition. Southern whites and Negroes did not worship together. Had such been attempted in the South, the result would have been bitter resentment among the white non-Pentecostals. This, in turn, could have seriously handicapped the future ministry of these Southern preachers and their churches. For this reason, General Conferences of the Pentecostal Assemblies of the World, excepting the first after the merger, were always held in the North.

But this, too, posed a problem. Many Southern ministers found it extremely difficult to travel the great distance to these

---

[3] McClain, Unpublished Notes.
[4] Ibid.

Northern meetings, year after year. Because of this, they had little representation in the affairs of the organization. All this led to a great deal of dissatisfaction.

The Southern Bible Conference

It seems necessary to report this meeting in detail, because of what it revealed, and what grew out of it.

This conference, held in Little Rock, Arkansas, November 3-12, 1922, was not an official meeting of the Pentecostal Assemblies of the World. But it was called by S. C. McClain, who had been a District Overseer of the organization for the state of Arkansas since 1920, and by Wm. A. Mulford. And the conference chairman was D. C. O. Opperman, who was a minister in the Pentecostal Assemblies of the World, as were most of the other ministers who attended.

McClain and Mulford sent out a letter of invitation which read, in part:

> *"You will be glad that the South, this fall, is to have a gathering of all the real saints of God. A great Bible conference will be held for all the Southern states....*
>
> *"Our purpose in calling such a meeting is to work for greater unity; we all need one another . . . The South has long looked for and hoped for true fellowship and unity, and we believe this meeting will do a great deal to bring this about.*
>
> *"This is not to be the beginning of a new movement, but a gathering of God's people where all can feel perfect fellowship in the Spirit of God. We desire to fill a vacancy left in other gatherings, and, through the Holy Spirit, be able to love one another as He has loved us."*[5]

It is easy to see, from this letter, that in the hearts of these men there was a longing for something that they had

[5] Ibid.

not found in meetings of the Pentecostal Assemblies of the World.

Between 60 and 70 ministers, most of whom were from the Southern states, attended the meeting. From all descriptions, surely it was one of the most glorious gatherings of Pentecostal ministers and laymen in modern times. Business was practically forgotten. During the entire series of services, the main emphasis was upon the need of the ministry for prayer, consecration, and a closer walk with God.

Wm. E. Booth-Clibborn thought the services so glorious that he preserved the memory of them in a book entitled, *A Call to Dust and Ashes.* (The author is indebted to Ralph G. Cook for the privilege of reading his copy of this book.) Booth-Clibborn described the conference as ". . . the best and most beneficial conference I have attended on the American continent for the past ten years."

He continued, "Meetings were held three times daily; food was forgotten, along with sleep. The realities of things unseen were overwhelming. There was a Communion service for preachers which lasted until 3:00 a. m. It seems it just couldn't be brought to an end."

Ralph G. Cook, later to become an Assistant General Superintendent of the United Pentecostal Church, was then pastor of the church in which the conference was held. Known far and wide for his keen sense of humor, as well as for his piety, he tells this amusing story on himself:

"As pastor, I had been out buying supplies for the meeting. I came into the church, walked up on the platform, and took the seat I usually occupied. Brother Opperman, who had charge of the services, said to me, 'Young man, when you come into a feast, you are to take the lower seat. There are more worthy men sitting behind you.' I humbly moved, though I was pastor. Later, Brother Opperman came to me, feeling that his remark had hurt me, and told me not to backslide over what he had said."

The 1923 General Conference

Because the Southern Bible Conference had been such a blessing, it was suggested that the first two days of the 1923 General Conference be given over to a similar meeting.

Comments McClain: "This had all the appearance of forcing the Southern Bible Conference to become an integral part of the convention. For this, the Southern ministers were blamed.

"Our brethren made the mistake of not thinking how it would sound to use the word 'Southern' in this Northern meeting. Then, too, I was elected chairman of this part of the conference. This was a mistake, as it gave the Negro ministers the wrong impression of the purpose of the meeting. Thus our effort to promote a good thing failed, and contributed further to the decision of the white ministers to leave the Pentecostal Assemblies of the World." [6]

The Separation Draws Nearer

From September 30 to October 3, 1924, the Pentecostal Assemblies of Texas, a district of the Pentecostal Assemblies of the World, met in Houston, Texas for their annual meeting.

Their first order of business was the adopting of a resolution to begin publishing, in Pt. Arthur, Texas, a four-page district paper, to be called *The Pentecostal Witness*. O. F. Fauss was chosen Editor.

In this meeting the three following questions were raised, and answered:

1. Should the name of the general body be changed from Pentecostal Assemblies of the World to the Pentecostal Assemblies of Jesus Only? It was decided that the name should be changed to the Pentecostal Assemblies of Jesus Christ.[7] Two things should be noted here: First, to many ministers, the word "World" in the organizational name had always

---

[6] Ibid.

[7] Pentecostal Witness, November, 1924 p. 4.

been unpopular; second, the name suggested as a replacement would be used to designate an organization that would be formed seven years later.

2. Should the present form of government be so changed that the one body would continue as a unit, yet be under separate managements, one for the white race and one for the Colored race, each to have and to maintain its own separate places of worship, its own ministers, its own responsibilities, its own boards, but cooperate together in some plan for general counsel and foreign missionary work? The group voted that the form of government should be changed.[8]

3. What should be done about Sunday school literature? Ministers at the conference voted to urge that the organization take steps to provide ". . . our people with Jesus' Only literature."[9]

It was not the intention of these ministers to completely break away from the Pentecostal Assemblies of the World, for J. R. Shinn was appointed as a delegate to attend the 1924 General Convention, scheduled to meet in Chicago on October 14. He also carried a letter from the Texas ministers, asking that he be re-appointed District Elder for 1925.[10]

The 1924 General Conference

This was the ninth annual conference of the Pentecostal Assemblies of the World.

Of this meeting, Andrew D. Urshan, who had been appointed Foreign Missionary Secretary in 1923, wrote: ". . . our delegation from the Southern states brought before the conference some timely and important matters pertaining to the civil laws in the South, which were rather hindering the work of the Lord in its proper and extensive progress."[11]

---

[8] Ibid.
[9] Ibid.
[10] Ibid.
[11] Ibid., December, 1924, p. 2

W. E. Kidson, soon to become prominent among Oneness Pentecostals, added these words: "It was the general opinion that this (the problems arising in the interracial organization) was a hindrance to the spreading of the gospel. For several years it had been talked, pro and con, about separation, not on doctrinal lines, but on racial lines.

"Still, the majority of the brethren everywhere were opposed to complete separation. During the convention, it was first proposed to the General Board of Presbyters that there be an Eastern and a Western division, the one to be exclusively Colored, and the other exclusively white — each to issue credentials to its own people. This proposal was rejected by the General Presbyters.

"There seemed nothing to do, then, but for the white brethren, who felt that their ministry was hindered, to separate from the Pentecostal Assemblies of the World. This was done, not because of a feeling against any other race, but only to help spread the glorious gospel." [12]

A Preliminary Meeting

Ministers interested in forming a new organization were asked to meet in a separate room. They met on October 16, 17. Present were Howard A. Goss, Andrew D. Urshan, Wm. E. Booth-Clibborn, W. E. Kidson, A. D. Gurley, and others.

The meeting was called to order by H. A. Goss. W. E. Kidson was chosen temporary Chairman. A. D. Gurley was chosen temporary Secretary.

It was decided that the new organization should be called "The Apostolic Churches of Jesus Christ."

Seven Presbyters were to be elected to make up the Executive Head. They were to appoint, from their number, a Chairman, a Secretary-Treasurer, and a Foreign Missionary Secretary-Treasurer.

---

[12] The Apostolic Herald, July, 1930, p. 5

Fields of labor in the organization were to be divided into Districts, each District to be presided over by a District Elder.

Elected as Presbyters, to serve only until the first organizational meeting, were J. C. Brickey, A. D. Urshan, W. E. Kidson, W. D. McBryde, G. C. Lout, H. A. Goss, and D. C. O. Opperman. They were to prepare Articles of Faith and a set of bylaws to govern the organization, and were to present them at the special conference, in which the new organization would be formed.[13]

Thus, after working in the interracial Pentecostal Assemblies of the World for approximately seven years, the white ministers took steps to form an organization of their own.

---

[13] Pentecostal Witness, December, 1924, p. 2

4

The Pentecostal Ministerial Alliance

The last part of chapter three told how certain ministers of the Pentecostal Assemblies of the World met during their conference in Chicago, in October, 1924, and took steps to form a new, all-white organization. A special conference was to be held later to set up the organization.

The group met at the old Lexington Avenue Church in Jackson, Tennessee, where J. C. Brickey was pastor, February 17-27, 1925.[1] Howard A. Goss was elected temporary chairman. After a time of prayer, Goss and others in the group expressed their ideas concerning the kind of organization needed.[2]

According to T. C. Davis, first editor of the Apostolic Herald (the new organization's official voice), the work of organizing was not completed until a second meeting, held in St. Louis.[3] This was the first General Assembly of the movement, and it began November 3, 1925.[4]

Choosing A Name

In their 1924 Chicago meeting, the ministers had voted to call the new organization the Apostolic Churches of Jesus

---

[1] Supplement to Pentecostal Witness, April, 1925.
[2] Apostolic Herald, March, 1927, pp. 4, 5.
[3] Ibid., August, 1926, p. 4.
[4] Pentecostal Witness, October, 1925, p. 4.

Christ. But at the Jackson meeting it was decided to call it the Pentecostal Ministerial Alliance.

During the St. Louis meeting, they again voted to call the organization the Apostolic Churches of Jesus Christ, only to find that, in the time between the February and November conferences, W. H. Whittington had incorporated and chartered another group under that name.

Because of this, the General Board met later in St. Paul, Minnesota, and passed the following: "Resolved that the resolution passed at the St. Louis convention changing the name of the Pentecostal Ministerial Alliance to the Apostolic Churches of Jesus Christ be repealed, and that the former name be retained." [5]

Stating the reason for the name, Pentecostal Ministerial Alliance, W. E. Kidson, later to become General secretary, said, ". . . since we are only a body of ministers, the word MINISTERIAL is a proper title. And since we are allied together, no other word so fully describes us as ALLIANCE. Then we realize that for years we have been known as PENTECOSTAL people. Therefore, the name PENTECOSTAL MINISTERIAL ALLIANCE comes nearer explaining who and what we are, and what we stand for, than most any other name could." [6]

THE GENERAL ORGANIZATION

The Pentecostal Ministerial Alliance needed little organizational machinery in the beginning, since the group had only 222 ministers listed in its 1926–27 Ministerial Record.

The General Assembly

This was the name of the organization's annual general meeting until 1929, when it was changed to General Conference. This assemblage was the final authority in all matters.

---

[5] Minute Book, 1926-27, Resolution No. 19, p. 8.
[6] Apostolic Herald, April, 1927, p. 6.

Decisions of the various boards were brought before it for ratification, general officials were elected, and other business transacted.

Dates and places of General Conferences are listed below.

1925 – St. Louis, Missouri – November 3 –
1926 – St. Louis, Missouri – October 25 – 31
1927 – Indianapolis, Indiana – October 1 – 10
1928 – Little Rock, Arkansas – October 4 – 14
1929 – Shreveport, Louisiana – October 17 – 27
1930 – St. Louis, Missouri – October 16 – 26
1931 – St. Louis, Missouri – October 15 – 25
1932 – Little Rock, Arkansas – October 20 – 30

The Board of Presbyters

In the organization's bylaws it was stated that "The Executive Government of this body shall be vested in brethren to be called the Presbytery, who shall be elected by a majority vote of the General Assembly."[7] The Presbytery was to be made up of seven men, elected for a term of one year.[8]

Originally, the responsibilities and duties of the Presbytery were few. They looked after the general work of the organization. They elected District Presbyters for those areas which were not sufficiently organized to elect their own.

The Executive Board

Executive officers were to be the General Chairman, General Secretary-Treasurer, and Foreign Missionary Secretary. These three officials were to be elected from among the seven Presbyters, either by the Presbytery or the General Assembly.[9]

In 1930, at the General Conference, it was voted to have an Executive Board comprised of the General Superintendent,

---

[7] Ibid., p. 6.
[8] Ibid., p. 7.
[9] Ibid., p. 6.

General Conference of the Pentecostal Ministerial Alliance, held in Shreveport, Louisiana, October 17–27, 1929.

the General Secretary-Treasurer, and the General Sunday School Superintendent. This Executive Board, together with seven other elected members of the Presbytery, would make up a ten-member General Board.[10]

The General Chairman

This title was changed to General Superintendent at the 1929 General Conference.[11]

The Pentecostal Ministerial Alliance never had a full-time General Chairman (or Superintendent). The main duty of the General Superintendent was to preside over meetings of the General Conference. He did occasionally visit the various areas of the work, but his time for this was limited, since he was a full-time pastor.

In its eighth General Conference, in 1932, the organization voted to abolish the office of General Superintendent.[12] As this was also the meeting in which the group changed its name to Pentecostal Church, Incorporated, more will be said in chapter eight concerning this change in governmental structure.

DISTRICT ORGANIZATION

District Presbyters

District organization moved ahead slowly in the Pentecostal Ministerial Alliance. In many parts of the country its constituents were too few to justify the forming of districts.

At the Jackson meeting in 1925 this resolution was passed: "The field of labor shall be divided into districts, and an overseer elected from each district, who shall be called a District Presbyter." [13]

In the beginning, there were seven District Presbyters,

[10] Ibid., November, 1930, p. 5.
[11] Ibid., November, 1929, p. 6.
[12] Ibid., November, 1932, p. 9.
[13] Ibid., January, 1926, p. 6.

all elected at the General Assembly.[14] Later, as each new district was properly organized, it was allowed to elect its own District Presbyter at a District Council (Conference). However, District Presbyters to oversee the work in unorganized areas were still elected at the General Assembly.[15]

The first seven District Presbyters elected were from Arkansas, Idaho, Indiana, Louisiana, Missouri, Tennessee, and Wisconsin.[16]

A Premature Attempt

It was not until the fifth annual General Conference, held in 1929, that the group attempted to organize into clearly-defined districts. In this meeting they created nine different districts (also called regions): Eastern, Central, South-Central, Southeastern, Pacific Coast, and Northwestern (in the United States); and Eastern, Central, and Western (in Canada). [17] There seems no use to list the various states in these different districts, since the plan was soon discarded.

If the organizing of the aforementioned districts had been fully consummated, each District Presbyter would automatically have become a member of the General Board.[18] *Note: To the credit of these organizational pioneers, the United Pentecostal Church later adopted this method of choosing General Presbyters (District Superintendents).*

During 1930, Howard A. Goss, General Superintendent, organized five of the prescribed districts.[19]

But the plan, though good, was apparently premature. At the 1930 General Conference, held in St. Louis, October 16 – 26, it was resolved, ". . . that the regional plan adopted at Shreveport be repealed." In its stead, smaller districts

[14] Ibid.
[15] Ibid.
[16] Ibid.
[17] Ibid., December, 1929, p. 11.
[18] Apostolic Herald, November, 1929, p. 6.
[19] Ibid., July, 1930, p. 10.

were to be created throughout the continent, as the need arose.[20] The number of District Presbyters soon increased to twelve.

In its eighth General Conference, held in Little Rock, Arkansas, October, 1932, a district policy for governing the districts was adopted. As already stated, in that same meeting the organization changed its name to Pentecostal Church, Incorporated, so the implementation of the policy was left to this newly-named group.

GENERAL OFFICIALS

When the Pentecostal Ministerial Alliance was organized in February, 1925, L. C. Hall became its first Chairman, and Howard Goss its first Secretary. The seven General Presbyters were L. C. Hall, H. A. Goss, J. C. Brickey, Wm. A. Mulford, L. R. Ooton, W. D. McBryde, and A. D. Urshan.[21]

In the organization's first General Assembly, held in St. Louis the following November, Howard Goss became Chairman, and L. R. Ooton was elected Secretary. The five additional General Presbyters were T. C. Davis, J. C. Brickey, J. A. Frush, W. E. Kidson, and W. H. Lyon.[22] *Note: One wonders if Lyon was not absent from this meeting, and elected a General Presbyter without his knowledge. Approximately two weeks before this time he had helped organize Emmanuel's Church in Jesus Christ, in Houston, Texas, and had been elected its first Chairman. (See page 54.)*

L. R. Ooton resigned as Secretary in October, 1928, and W. E. Kidson was chosen to succeed him.[23]

In March, 1932, Howard Goss resigned as General Superintendent, stating that he desired to devote full time to his

---

[20] Ibid., November, 1930, p. 5.
[21] Supplement to Pentecostal Witness, April, 1925.
[22] Apostolic Herald, January, 1926, p. 7.
[23] Ibid., November, 1928, p. 6.

church in Toronto, Canada.[24] No successor was chosen, for, as already stated, the office was abolished that same year in October.

MEMBERSHIP

For the Ministry

To affiliate with the Pentecostal Ministerial Alliance, a minister had to fill out an application, and have it endorsed by a Presbyter who knew him. When this was properly passed upon, he was granted a license or credential.

In the beginning, a new application was filled out, and a new license or credential issued, each year. W. E. Kidson stated the reason for this: "As you know, some ministers change their doctrines, and do not stay with the truth, so the easiest way for us to find this out, and to keep an accurate record, is to have a new application properly filled out each year."[25] This requirement was soon dropped, and a new license or credential was automatically issued each year.

At the General Conference in St. Louis, in October, 1930, it was decided to have two classes of ordained ministers. One would first be ordained as a local minister. Then after he had gained "a great deal of experience, and had fully proven himself," he would be given full ordination. This latter ordination was to take place only at a General Conference.[26]

This procedure was changed at the next General Conference. There it was decided that a Local License would be issued to local workers. Then after one had labored faithfully, in cooperation with some assembly, for one year or more, a General License would be given. Finally, when one had met the requirements, and had been ordained, he would be given a full credential.[27] This same plan of ministerial membership,

---

[24] Ibid., July, 1932, p. 4.
[25] Ibid., January, 1929, p. 15.
[26] Ibid., November, 1930, p. 6.
[27] Ibid., November, 1931, p. 7.

in an extended form, was later adopted by the United Pentecostal Church.

The first ministerial membership fee was $5 per year.[28] In the 1929 General Assembly it was voted that each minister send in $12 annually, and that each assembly take an offering once each year, for the support of headquarters.[29]

For Local Churches

It was established early in this chapter that the Pentecostal Ministerial Alliance, as the name implies, was only a body of ministers.

But as early as January, 1926, a change was already noticeable. Said Howard Goss: "The word ministerial does not mean that assemblies (local churches) are not cared for or protected, for they are. A provision is made for their fellowship and cooperation."[30]

In 1928, at the fourth General Assembly, a resolution was adopted that all assemblies affiliated with the Pentecostal Ministerial Alliance should be listed in the Minute Book for 1929, and that a letter of recognition should be sent to each affiliated assembly.[31]

It was not until 1930 that any restrictions were placed upon local assemblies desiring fellowship with the organization. That year it was decided to impose the following requirements: ". . . Any assembly may be in cooperation with, and under the protection of, the Pentecostal Ministerial Alliance by adopting the fundamentals and bylaws, and sending a letter of notification to the General Secretary."[32]

In its eighth General Conference, held in Little Rock, Arkansas, October 20–30, 1932, the organization adopted

[28] Ibid., April, 1929, p. 9.
[29] Ibid., November, 1929, p. 6.
[30] Ibid., January, 1926, p. 4.
[31] Ibid., November, 1928, p. 6.
[32] Ibid., April, 1930, p. 4.

a lengthy and detailed form of local church government.[33] Apparently it served its purpose well, for it was accepted (with minor changes) by the United Pentecostal Church in 1945, and has continued in use through the years.

With the forming of this policy, the organization changed completely from a ministerial alliance to one that included local churches.

DEPARTMENTS

Departments in the Pentecostal Ministerial Alliance were few, and simply organized. As in the case of districts, there was little need for departmental organization.

Foreign Missions

Foreign missionary activity in the movement was first mentioned in this declaration: ". . . the foreign missionary cause shall be recognized by the Pentecostal Ministerial Alliance as of equal importance with home missionary work."[34]

E. C. Steinberg, formerly a missionary to China, was chosen first Foreign Missionary Secretary-Treasurer in 1927.[35]

Foreign missionaries supported either wholly or partially by the organization at various times were: L. W. Coote, Japan; L. H. Dickson, Jerusalem; C. M. and Mabel Hensley, China; A. J. and Pearl Holmes, Liberia; Mae Iry, India; Elsie King, China; Alice Kugler (later Sheets), China; Garland and Eleanor Leonard, China; Dorothy McCarty, India; A. O. Moore, India; Joseph Rezniczek, India; Elizabeth Steiglitz, China; J. B. Thomas, Jerusalem; and Timothy Urshan, Jerusalem.

Foreign missionary offerings for 1929, the first year of which we have a record, totaled $3,090.91.[36] Offerings increased little in the following three years, but one must remember that this was the time of "The Depression."

---

[33] Ibid., November, 1932, pp. 10, 11, 12.
[34] Ibid., November, 1927, p. 3.
[35] Ibid.
[36] Ibid., January – December, 1929.

Sunday School

The name Dan Hayes is familiar to most Oneness Pentecostal people whose experience dates back to the 1930's and 1940's. Formerly a Methodist minister, he first affiliated with Emmanuel's Church in Jesus Christ, and became State Sunday School Superintendent for the state of Louisiana in 1926. (See page 56.)

Hayes left this organization in 1927, and became a member of the Pentecostal Ministerial Alliance. In October of that same year he was appointed General Sunday School Organizer for this group.[37]

In this capacity, he traveled throughout the United States, assisting local Sunday schools in organizing, and in increasing their efficiency. He was highly commended for this work.

Later, General Sunday School Conventions were held at General Conferences, the first three days being set aside for this purpose.

Hayes was to remain active in Sunday School work in the Pentecostal Church, Incorporated, and for a time in the United Pentecostal Church, until his death in 1949.

At its fourth General Assembly, held in October, 1928, the Pentecostal Ministerial Alliance adopted a brief National Sunday School Policy, and formed a loosely-knit National Sunday School Department.

In each state where the organization had sufficient assemblies to justify it, there was to be a state Sunday School Superintendent, an Assistant Superintendent, and a Secretary-Treasurer. State Superintendents were appointed in eleven states, and one in Canada.[38]

The year following, in the group's fifth General Assembly, a Sunday School Board was elected, to help implement the Sunday School Policy. This board consisted of the Sunday

---

[37] Ibid., October, November, 1927, p. 12.
[38] Ibid., November, 1928, p. 7.

School Superintendent, and two additional members, with power to act in all matters pertaining to Sunday school work of the organization.[39]

Youth

Perhaps the first step toward organized youth work in the Pentecostal Ministerial Alliance was the appointing of W. A. Mulford as General Organizer ". . . for the Young People's Alliance."

Any assembly desiring his help was asked to get in touch with him. He had a set of bylaws that were recommended as beneficial to youth work. (We have no record of the formulating of these bylaws, or of what they contained.)

Officials of the organization declared, "It is our desire to push this part of the work throughout the world." [40]

The youth work was more fully organized in the General Assembly of 1929, with the passing of a resolution that ". . . we hereby provide for coordinating the work of our young people by forming an international organization, to be known as the Pentecostal Young People's Alliance." [41]

At the 1930 General Conference, held in St. Louis, the name of the youth organization was changed to Pentecostal Gleaners.[42] A brief policy was adopted.[43] Ralph Glasgow was elected President, and Danita Barnum, Secretary. They continued to serve through the remainder of the Pentecostal Ministerial Alliance's history.

The name "Pentecostal Gleaners" carried over into the Pentecostal Church, Incorporated, and was used until that group ceased to exist in 1945.

---

[39] Ibid., November, 1929, p. 6.
[40] Ibid. p. 7.
[41] Ibid.
[42] Ibid., March, 1932, p. 4.
[43] Ibid., November, 1930, p. 5.

DOCTRINE

The first published statement, relative to the doctrinal position of the Pentecostal Ministerial Alliance, was this: "The Bible way of salvation is repentance toward God, faith toward our Lord Jesus Christ, obedience to the Word of God by baptism in water (in Jesus' name), and receiving the gift of the Holy Ghost, as in Acts 2:4, 38." [44]

The main doctrinal requirements for ministerial membership in the organization were that one must be filled with the Holy Ghost, with the evidence of speaking with other tongues; must teach the same; and must have been baptized, and baptize, in Jesus' name. [45]

Howard Goss, General Superintendent, made this statement: "We hold that the Christian church began on the day of Pentecost, and to be in that body, one must be baptized in the Holy Spirit." [46]

In 1930, George R. Farrow, well-known minister and author, wrote an article entitled, "The New Birth—What It Is; What It Does," in which he said, "First we wish to state that being born of water and of the Spirit, and being baptized in water and with the Spirit, mean one and the same thing. For if being baptized in water and the Spirit, as in Acts 2:38, is not the birth that Jesus referred to in the third chapter of St. John, then we will search the New Testament in vain for the description of an experience which is that. . . ." [47]

Of course, there were others in the Pentecostal Ministerial Alliance who did not agree with these statements made by Farrow. (This will be brought out more fully in chapter eight, which concerns the same group, after its name was changed to the Pentecostal Church, Incorporated.)

---

[44] Ibid., January, 1926, p. 6.
[45] Ibid., July, 1930, p. 5.
[46] Ibid., September, 1929, p. 8.
[47] Ibid., August, 1930, p. 3.

BASIS OF MINISTERIAL FELLOWSHIP

If one wonders how ministers of such different doctrinal beliefs could work together in one movement, let it be remembered that the Pentecostal Ministerial Alliance was organized upon this very basis. Divergent doctrinal views were allowed, so long as a minister subscribed to the doctrinal fundamentals set forth in paragraph two, under DOCTRINE.

In the Preamble to the Constitution one finds these words: "We shall endeavor to keep the unity of the Spirit in the bond of peace with all the Spirit-filled saints of God, until we all come to the unity of the faith. To this end, we pledge our prayers, our faith, our lives and love, our means and time, in the fear of God, and for His glory alone." [48]

Howard Goss said, "We have principles to stand for, but we are trying not to be narrow or sectarian. The emphasis is to be placed upon a clean life, and not so much on special doctrine. Though we do not compromise, and though we have convictions of our own, we will not force our convictions on our brethren, but let love, as well as doctrine, be the chief factor in governing the conduct of all." [49]

The organization recognized that some of its ministers had doctrines that were dear to themselves, and seemed essential. These ministers were not to be hindered in preaching their views in their own assemblies, but were not to preach such doctrines in other assemblies without the consent of the pastor in charge.[50] (Do not forget that the doctrines mentioned in this paragraph were other than the basic ones required for membership in the organization.)

PUBLICATIONS

The Apostolic Herald

In its first General Assembly, held in St. Louis in Novem-

---

[48] Ibid., January, 1926, p. 6.
[49] Ibid., p. 4.
[50] Ibid., July, 1930, p. 5.

ber, 1925, the Pentecostal Ministerial Alliance decided to publish an official paper: "In order that all Spirit-filled brethren everywhere might know more about one another, and that we might have a better way of helping spread the glorious news concerning the work." The paper was to be called The Apostolic Herald.[51] It was published bimonthly through 1926, and monthly thereafter.

T. C. Davis became the first editor, and W. E. Kidson, the managing editor. Davis resigned in 1927, and J. A. Frush succeeded him. At the 1929 General Assembly, Frush resigned, and Kidson was chosen editor.

Beginning as an eight-page periodical, the paper was enlarged to sixteen pages in March, 1928. Circulation also increased, and by the end of 1929 had reached approximately 8,000.[52]

Sunday School Literature

The Pentecostal Ministerial Alliance had been in existence for more than three years before it took steps to begin publishing Sunday school literature.

In its 1928 General Assembly it was decided to try to have Sunday school literature ready in time for the second quarter of 1929. Ethel E. Goss was appointed editor. The literature was to be published in Toronto, Canada, where she lived.[53]

It was not until the second quarter of 1930, however, that the new literature was available. W. E. Kidson said, "We are now ready with the literature. We have our own Junior, Intermediate and Adult quarterlies." [54]

Perhaps some will smile when they compare later Sunday school literature with these three small quarterlies. But let us not despise the day of small things. This was the first time

[51] Ibid., January, 1926, p. 4.
[52] Ibid., January, 1930, p. 4.
[53] Ibid., December, 1928, p. 11.
[54] Kidson, Apostolic Herald, March, 1930, p. 16.

that a Oneness organization had published its own Sunday school literature.

HEADQUARTERS

The Pentecostal Ministerial Alliance was incorporated in the state of Missouri, and its headquarters was at Louisiana, Missouri. This was the hometown of W. E. Kidson, who, you will recall, was managing editor of the Apostolic Herald, which was printed in Louisiana.

Kidson was apparently the only official of the organization who ever lived in the headquarters city. In the 1929 General Assembly it was voted that General Superintendent Howard Goss should move to headquarters, and give his full time to work on the field.[55] Goss was, at this time, pastor in Toronto, Canada. There is no record that he moved to headquarters.

GROWTH

When the Pentecostal Ministerial Alliance was organized at Jackson, Tennessee, in 1925, approximately 60 ministers became charter members.[56]

Sometimes ministers affiliated with the organization in groups. For instance, in May, 1926, the Oneness ministers of Tennessee voted to join the movement. The Chairman was H. G. Rodgers, who was mentioned in chapter one, in connection with the coming of Oneness to the state.[57]

As stated earlier in this chapter, ministerial membership had reached 222 by 1926. During 1929, the membership of the organization doubled.[58]

In May, 1932, W. E. Kidson said, "More than 100 ministers have affiliated with us since our General Conference in October, 1931."[59]

[55] Ibid., December, 1929, p. 4.
[56] Letter from A. D. Gurley.
[57] Ibid., June, 1926, p. 8.
[58] Ibid., January, 1930, p. 4.
[59] Ibid., May, 1932, p. 4.

It is regrettable that more information is not available concerning the numerical strength of the organization. Such figures have always been hard to obtain from Oneness Pentecostals.

THE LAST CONFERENCE

The Pentecostal Ministerial Alliance held its last General Conference (the eighth) in 1932. Further history of the group, as the Pentecostal Church, Incorporated, will be found in chapter eight.

5

Emmanuel's Church in Jesus Christ

The preceding chapter of this work dealt with the founding and subsequent history of the Pentecostal Ministerial Alliance.

That organization was established with high hopes. Howard A. Goss said shortly thereafter, "We trust that the Pentecostal Ministerial Alliance will be what many Pentecostal ministers are desiring in the way of fellowship."[1] W. D. McBryde, speaking of the desire of many for a suitable organization, said, "They hope they have found it in the Pentecostal Ministerial Alliance."[2]

But some of the ministers who had left the Pentecostal Assemblies of the World were dissatisfied with the newly-formed organization. This is seen in their forming of another — Emmanuel's Church in Jesus Christ — eight months later.[3]

Why the Dissatisfaction?

Why were these ministers, some few of whom had shortly before assisted in forming the Pentecostal Ministerial Alliance, now dissatisfied with it?

Different reasons were stated, but the main one was this: They declared that the Pentecostal Ministerial Alliance "... was so organized to only look after and care for ministers,

---

[1] Apostolic Herald, January, 1926, p. 4.

[2] Supplement to Pentecostal Witness, April, 1925.

[3] Fauss, Pentecostal Witness, November, 1926, p. 4.

and the saints had no protection, and no form of church government."[4] For this reason, the group desired to form a *church* organization, rather than simply a ministerial association or alliance.

Forming the New Organization

In 1925 the Trio States Camp Meeting was held October 15–25, in Houston, Texas. (The trio states were Texas, Louisiana, and Oklahoma.)

On October 21, approximately fifty ministers and Christian workers assembled in a business meeting. They began the proceedings by raising the question: "What is the main purpose of this meeting?" In reply, it was stated that the purpose was to form, in the fear of God, an organization that would serve the cause of God everywhere, especially in the South, more satisfactorily than other organizations had done.

W. H. Lyon of Comanche, Texas was appointed chairman pro tem, and G. C. Stroud, secretary.[5]

Naming the Organization

The second matter brought up in the meeting was that of choosing a proper and Scriptural name for the new organization. The name Apostolic Church (or churches) of Jesus Christ was extremely popular among Oneness Pentecostal people at that time, so it was decided to use the name Apostolic Churches of Jesus Christ.[6] You will notice later in this chapter that the name became Apostolic *Church* of Jesus Christ.

The group soon encountered difficulty concerning the name it had chosen. Oliver F. Fauss said, "After we had chosen the name Apostolic Churches of Jesus Christ, and proceeded to have the movement chartered under that name, we found

---

[4] Pentecostal Witness, January, 1927, p. 2.

[5] Pentecostal Witness, November, 1925, p. 4.

[6] Ibid.

that a group (in St. Louis) had already chartered a movement under that name (see page 36), therefore the law would not permit us to present a charter under the same name. Upon obtaining this information, a number of brethren, both in Louisiana and Texas, were consulted, and the name Emmanuel's Church in Jesus Christ was chosen, and heartily endorsed by these brethren." [7]

But the group was never satisfied with this name, as will be seen by a later statement.

Two more business meetings were required, on October 22 and 23, for the forming of the new organization.

CHURCH POLITY

The charter members of Emmanuel's Church in Jesus Christ decided that the organization should be governed by a board of twelve ministers. A Chairman, a Secretary-Treasurer, and a Foreign Missions Secretary-Treasurer would be elected from among the twelve, for a term of one year.

W. H. Lyon was elected Chairman, and G. C. Stroud was chosen Secretary-Treasurer. Andrew D. Urshan was the Foreign Missions Secretary-Treasurer.

Each presbyter was granted the right to organize a state board in his state, if no state organization had already been formed. He was, further, to encourage the work in those states which were already properly organized. [8]

Women were ordained in Emmanuel's Church of Jesus Christ, but the movement did not permit them to take charge of business matters in the churches. [9]

MEMBERSHIP

Emmanuel's Church in Jesus Christ was formed by ministers who had left the interracial Pentecostal Assemblies of the World in 1924. But in the organization conference they

[7] Pentecostal Witness, February, 1926, p. 1.
[8] Ibid., November, 1925, p. 4.
[9] Ibid., May, 1927, p. 4.

passed a resolution that, since the new movement included those of all nations, irrespective of color, race or class, the Colored brethren who desired to fellowship and cooperate with the new movement would be granted full rights. Then, when their number increased sufficiently to merit a separate Colored work, they would be granted the privilege of organizing their own movement, with their own officials and headquarters, according to their God-given wish. Even then, however, they were to work in harmony with the main headquarters, which would be governed by white ministers.[10]

The latter part of the preceding sentence sets forth one difference between this new organization and the Pentecostal Assemblies of the World, which had been governed by both Negroes and whites.

DEPARTMENTS

Departmental organization on a national scale was practically nonexistent in Emmanuel's Church in Jesus Christ. This was due partially to the short time that the movement continued before it merged with another group, and changed its name. The main reason, however, for this lack was that there were not enough churches and ministers in some areas to merit such organization.

Foreign Missions

As already stated, Andrew D. Urshan was elected first Foreign Missions Secretary of the group. The fact that they formed such an office in their organization conference showed that they were foreign missionary minded.

Every church was asked to receive a foreign missionary offering on the second Sunday of each month. These offerings were small, but so were all offerings in those days. The organization helped support the following missionaries: A. Reynolds; R. B. Sonnenberg; G. M. Cound; Mae Iry; Alice S. Kugler (all

---

[10] Ibid., November, 1925.

in China); Dorothy L. McCarty; Wm. McGregor; Henrietta Wise (all in India); Leonard Coote, Japan; and Timothy Urshan, Jerusalem.

Sunday School

The organization had no national Sunday school department.

Apparently some of its ministers and laymen showed little interest in Sunday school. This was the opinion of Dan Hayes, Sunday school editor of the Pentecostal Witness, and State Sunday School Superintendent for Louisiana. Hayes, later to become widely known among Oneness Pentecostals for his intense interest in Sunday school work, said, "... There are people in this movement who think we should attend only night services . . . Brethren, where are your boys and girls spending their Sundays? The Sunday school is the school of Christ for the church, not a side issue." [11]

A Sunday school convention was held in Eunice, Louisiana, June 11–13, 1926. So far as our records show, this was the first such convention held among Oneness Pentecostal people.

Youth

The young people of Emmanuel's Church in Jesus Christ were never organized nationally, though many of the local churches undoubtedly did have organized groups.

In 1927, Oliver F. Fauss, then pastor at Pt. Arthur, Texas, formed a local youth group in his church, and called it the Pentecostal Strivers. He suggested that other young people's groups adopt the same name. Fauss did this because many young people in different assemblies had expressed their desire for a young people's organization.[12]

Some few assemblies apparently complied with Fauss'

---

[11] Pentecostal Witness, June, 1926, p. 1.
[12] Ibid., September, 1927, p. 4.

request, but the movement evidently failed to gain wide acceptance.

PUBLICATIONS

The Pentecostal Witness

The Texas District of the Pentecostal Assemblies of the World had begun publishing this periodical as their official state paper in November, 1924. O. F. Fauss was the editor.

Naturally, when these ministers left the Pentecostal Assemblies of the World, they retained control of their district paper. Then, at the General Convention in August, 1926, it became the official organ of Emmanuel's Church in Jesus Christ.[13] At that time it had grown from four to eight pages.

Fauss served as editor for more than four years, and then asked to be replaced. He did a fine work as editor. Undoubtedly the paper did much to hold the young organization together, publicize its various activities, and "recruit" other ministers.

Sunday School Literature

From the beginning, Emmanuel's Church in Jesus Christ desired its own Sunday school literature. Fauss put this desire into words when he said, "We long to see the day when our organization will own a publishing house . . . where Sunday school literature preaching the message of the name of Jesus can be obtained." [14]

At the Southern Bible Conference, held in Merryville, Louisiana, February 4–12, 1927, a committee was appointed to work toward the producing of Oneness Pentecostal Sunday school literature.[15]

E. D. Browning was chosen Sunday School Superintendent in 1927, when Dan Hayes resigned. Browning was given permission to accept money toward the purchasing of a printing press on which to print Sunday school literature.

[13] Ibid., October, 1926, p. 4.
[14] Ibid.
[15] Ibid., March, 1927, p. 2.

Later, toward the end of its history as an organization, Emmanuel's Church in Jesus Christ thought it best to postpone the publishing of its own Sunday school literature. Browning was instructed to return to the contributors all money received for the Press Fund.[16]

HEADQUARTERS

Since the organization had been formed in the South, and as most of its ministers and churches were in the South, it was decided to establish the headquarters in Beaumont, Texas.

In addition, the group approved the idea of opening a branch office in the North, in a place to be chosen by the Northern brethren, to work with the Southern headquarters, until the Northern group was strong enough numerically to have a separate headquarters of its own, in order to spread the gospel in the North, East, and West.[17]

The idea of two separate headquarters seems strange to us today. But in those days, before the advent of modern air travel made nearly every part of the country easily and quickly accessible, ministers in the North would feel far removed from the Southern headquarters. Thus it was planned to have a separate headquarters in the North, when such became practicable.

Speaking of the headquarters, it was said, ". . . the office and equipment are all arranged for, and without debt." [18] Of course, the headquarters probably included only an office, with essential equipment.

GROWTH

Emmanuel's Church in Jesus Christ made steady progress. The Board of Presbyters issued this statement: "Brethren

---

[16] Ibid., December, 1928, p. 7.
[17] Ibid., November, 1925, p. 5.
[18] Ibid., January, 1927, p. 2.

from north, south, east and west, far and near, are expressing their gratitude for the organization, and are well pleased with its plans and principles. . . ." [19]

This acceptance led to satisfactory growth. The first ministerial list published showed 112 names. Date of publication is not given, but in April, 1927, it was said, ". . . the record has almost doubled, with only a half dozen withdrawals." [20]

A SIGNIFICANT MERGER

In this chapter, under Naming the Organization (page 53), mention was made of a St. Louis group which had chartered an organization known as the Apostolic Churches of Jesus Christ.

Emmanuel's Church in Jesus Christ first moved toward a merger with this group by asking for a joint convention, to be held in October, 1927.

In announcing this joint meeting, it was said, "This convention is for the main purpose of consolidating into one great body these two organizations, thus uniting near 400 Jesus only ministers. . . ." [21] It was reported that many other ministers, not affiliated with any organization, were looking favorably toward the convention, expecting to join the group if the merger were effected.

The joint convention was held in Guthrie, Oklahoma, October 18-22, 1927. There the two bodies voted to consolidate.

For some reason, not explained, it was decided to continue using the name Emmanuel's Church in Jesus Christ, though both groups certainly favored the name Apostolic Church (or Churches) of Jesus Christ.

Elected as officials of the organization, for a one-year term, were Ben Pemberton, Chairman; W. H. Lyon, Vice

[19] Ibid.
[20] Ibid., April, 1927, p. 2.
[21] Ibid., July, 1927, p. 1.

Chairman; W. H. Whittington, Secretary and Foreign Missionary Secretary; and J. O White, Treasurer.

The minute books (manuals) of the two groups were considered, and after discussing certain necessary changes, it was agreed to consolidate the two books into one. This was to be done by a committee, composed of Cleve Kerley, Oliver F. Fauss and C. A. Pyatt.[22]

The Merger Consummated

The work of consolidating the two organizations was not completed at the 1927 special joint meeting.

Steps to consummate the merger were taken at the next General Convention of Emmanuel's Church in Jesus Christ, held in Pt. Arthur, Texas, October 16-21, 1928.

At this convention, attended by approximately 80 ministers and workers from various parts of the country, ". . . Emmanuel's Church in Jesus Christ and the Apostolic Church of Jesus Christ successfully consolidated into one great body. Without a single voice against it, the convention voted to accept the name Apostolic Church of Jesus Christ for the general body. This was exactly the desire (so far as a name was concerned) of the brethren when Emmanuel's Church was first organized. We feel that the Lord has wonderfully brought this about in His own way." [23]

As the Pt. Arthur convention was attended by only a few of the ministers who had belonged to the pre-merger Apostolic Church of Jesus Christ, it was decided to elect officials for the coming year, subject to the approval of the St. Louis brethren in their annual convention, to be held in St. Louis, October 31, 1928. The following officials were elected: Oliver F. Fauss, Chairman; Ben Pemberton, Assistant Chairman; W. H. Whittington, Secretary; Maud Whittington, Assistant Secretary; and E. D. Browning, Treasurer, and Foreign Missions Secretary.

[22] Ibid., December, 1927, p. 8.
[23] Ibid., December, 1928, p. 1.

At the St. Louis meeting, the elected officials were approved.

In this meeting, the Apostolic Messenger, voice of the pre-merger Apostolic Church of Jesus Christ, was combined with the Pentecostal Witness, which, under this latter name, became the official voice of the merged group.[24]

Thus Emmanuel's Church in Jesus Christ ceased to exist as a separate body, after a brief history of three years.

---

[24] Ibid., p. 7.

6
The Apostolic Church of Jesus Christ

When the white ministers withdrew from the interracial Pentecostal Assemblies of the World in 1924, they established three Oneness organizations within the space of a year. The Pentecostal Ministerial Alliance was founded in February, 1925 (chapter 4). In October of that same year, Emmanuel's Church in Jesus Christ was started (chapter 5). The third organization, known as the Apostolic Churches of Jesus Christ, was begun in St. Louis by W. H. Whittington and Ben Pemberton, at about the same time as the Pentecostal Ministerial Alliance.

The latter part of chapter five told of the merging of this group with Emmanuel's Church in Jesus Christ. The merged group was known as the Apostolic Church of Jesus Christ.

In this chapter we shall continue the history of this amalgamated body.

Importance Attached to the Name

It was mentioned earlier in this work that Oneness Pentecostals highly favored the name Apostolic Church of Jesus Christ. In an article entitled "Is There Anything in the Name?" Maud Whittington, Assistant Secretary, explained why the name was so popular. She wrote: "We are made to believe that the name is now one of the most important things in regard to the establishing of the Apostolic Church of Jesus Christ.

"Why, then, call the organization by this name? Because the church is built upon the foundation of the apostles and prophets, Jesus Christ Himself being the chief corner stone. And because the church of Jesus Christ continued steadfastly in the apostles' doctrine." [1]

THE GENERAL ORGANIZATION

The history of the Apostolic Church of Jesus Christ was brief, covering only a three-year period after the merger. It had no organization other than that of a general (national) nature.

The General Convention

This meeting was held annually. A glance at the minutes will show that little business was transacted, other than the reading of minutes and financial reports, and the election of the few general officers of the organization.

General conventions and dates are shown below. These meetings actually date from the founding of both former organizations, hence the first convention listed is really the third.

1928 – St. Louis, Missouri – October 31 – November 3
1929 – Louann, Arkansas – October 8-13
1930 – Louann, Arkansas – September 29 – October 5
1931 – St. Louis, Missouri – October 6-11

There Was no Presbyter Board

In this, the Apostolic Church of Jesus Christ differed from all other Oneness organizations. Beginning in the Pentecostal Witness for December, 1930 the general officials were listed under Executive Board, but there is no record that they ever met as an official board.

It was not that the group just did not see the need of electing presbyters. Some, and apparently they were at first

---

[1] Pentecostal Witness, January, 1929, p. 2.

in the majority, were strongly opposed to having such officials.

W. H. Whittington, Editor and Secretary, wrote: "We have . . . a church strictly along Bible lines, and have taken a stand against unscriptural terms, and officers who are assigned sectional districts parceled out by controlling officers. . . ."[2]

Cleve Kerley, well-known evangelist in the group, said, "There are some who believe that the movement should be governed by a presbyter board, . . . but that doctrine is weighed in the balance, and found wanting. In the Bible, every duly ordained elder was a presbyter in the church of Christ."[3]

Later he wrote: "A General Presbyter means a presbyter over presbyters . . . There are no scriptures for a Board of Presbyters being elected by vote to govern and rule all the other presbyters . . . That's why the Apostolic Church of Jesus Christ has done away with presbyter boards."[4]

Not everyone in the organization agreed with this. And others apparently soon changed their minds. This is seen by the fact that within about fifteen months after Kerley wrote his last article opposing such, the group merged with the Pentecostal Assemblies of the World, and accepted the bylaw that there should be a board of *twenty-four* General Presbyters to govern the merged body.

The Chairman and Assistant Chairman

The Chairman did little, other than to preside over the General Convention.

Oliver F. Fauss was the first Chairman. He held the office from 1928 until 1930, when A. H. Beisner was elected to replace him. Beisner served until 1931.

Ben Pemberton was elected Assistant Chairman in 1928, and served until 1930, when Charles A. Smith was elected.

---

[2] Ibid., December, 1929, p. 3.
[3] Ibid., September, 1929, p. 5.
[4] Ibid., July – August, 1930, p. 7.

The Secretary

W. H. Whittington was the first Secretary of the Organization. He served from 1928 until 1930, when he was followed by L. R. Ooton. The secretarial duties were few, as were the duties of the Chairman.

The Treasurer

The first Treasurer of the organization was E. D. Browning. W. H. Whittington was elected Treasurer in 1930.

(Note: All the foregoing officials were elected at the General Convention, for a term of one year.)

DISTRICT ORGANIZATION

The Apostolic Church of Jesus Christ had no officially organized districts, though certain states having a larger number of constituents were sometimes called districts.

In the 1928 General Convention a resolution was passed "... to encourage each state or district to have camp meetings, ... for the advancement and upbuilding of the cause of Christ...." [5]

The first actual move toward district organization was made in the 1930 General Convention, when the group granted each state the privilege of self-government, so long as it did not conflict with the general policy of the organization.[6]

MINISTERIAL MEMBERSHIP

To affiliate with the Apostolic Church of Jesus Christ, a minister must fill out a blank, and send it to the Secretary, with a fee of $2, "... for the sole purpose of supporting the headquarters office." This had to be done annually, for all credentials were null and void without an annual certificate of fellowship attached.

The Secretary was instructed to reject "... any and all

---

[5] Ibid., December, 1928, p. 7.
[6] Ibid., December, 1930, p. 6.

applications for credentials not endorsed by three ordained ministers in fellowship with the Apostolic Church of Jesus Christ." [7]

FOREIGN MISSIONARY DEPARTMENT

As early as the 1928 General Convention, "The foreign missionary cause was discussed, and the matter of stirring up the interest for this cause among the people was encouraged." [8]

E. D. Browning served as Missionary Secretary throughout the organization's history.

The following missionaries were partially supported: *India* — Dorothy L. Mc Carty, Henry Tefre, Joseph Rezniczek; *China* — Mae Iry, Garland and Eleanor Leonard; *West Africa* — Pearl Holmes; *Jerusalem* — J. B. Thomas; and *Uruguay* — L. B. Sly

Missionary offerings were extremely small. From November 1, 1928 until October 1, 1929, total offerings were $122.[9]

DOCTRINAL POSITION

So far as the plan of salvation was concerned, the doctrinal position of the Apostolic Church of Jesus Christ was identical with that of the later-formed Pentecostal Assemblies of Jesus Christ, hence there seems no point in discussing its doctrinal position here. This is set forth in detail in chapter seven, pages 79, 80.

PUBLICATIONS

The Pentecostal Witness

This monthly periodical had been the official voice of the Texas District (Pentecostal Assemblies of the World). With the formation of Emmanuel's Church in Jesus Christ, it became the official organ of that group. Then, when Emmanuel's

[7] Ibid., December, 1928, p. 7.
[8] Ibid.
[9] Ibid., November, 1929, p. 4.

Church merged with the Apostolic Churches of Jesus Christ, the paper became the voice of the Apostolic Church of Jesus Christ.

In 1930 it was suggested that the name of the paper be changed to Apostolic Messenger, to better fit the organizational name, but this change was never made.[10]

At the time of the forming of the Apostolic Church of Jesus Christ, O. F. Fauss resigned as Editor, and W. H. Whittington succeeded him. The place of publication was moved from Pt. Arthur, Texas to St. Louis. James A. Frush became Editor in 1930, and the paper was then published in Newark, Ohio.

Note: The Apostolic Church of Jesus Christ published no Sunday school literature or other periodicals.

HEADQUARTERS

Headquarters for the organization existed more or less in name only. It was usually transferred to the city were the Secretary lived.

The first headquarters was in St. Louis, Missouri, at 1100 Hickory. In 1930, when L. R. Ooton became Secretary, headquarters was, in effect, moved to Akron, Ohio.

NUMERICAL STRENGTH

The Pentecostal Witness for December, 1929 listed 236 ministers as belonging to the Apostolic Church of Jesus Christ. Of this number, 25% was from Texas, almost 17% from Illinois, almost 17% from Missouri, 10% from Louisiana, and the remaining 31% from 15 other states.

During the days when there were two Oneness organizations, there was, of course, a certain amount of switching from one to another. Certain ministers in Texas and Louisiana had left Emmanuel's Church in Jesus Christ and affiliated with the Pentecostal Ministerial Alliance.[11] And ministers

---

[10] Ibid., December, 1930, pp. 4, 13.
[11] Foster, Think It Not Strange, p. 78.

in Ohio, belonging to the Tri State District Council, left the Pentecostal Ministerial Alliance, and united with the Apostolic Church of Jesus Christ.[12]

Such moves caused the numerical strength of the organization to fluctuate, but the overall picture was one of gradual growth.

ANOTHER MERGER

In chapter nine, entitled "Unsuccessful Attempts At Merger," there is an account of the Unity Conference, held at Columbus, Ohio in 1931. At this conference, a resolution was passed to bend every effort toward an amalgamation of all Jesus' name organizations.[13]

Seeking to implement this resolution, the Apostolic Church of Jesus Christ attempted to merge with the Pentecostal Ministerial Alliance. The attempt was unsuccessful.

When this occurred, the Apostolic Church of Jesus Christ turned to the Pentecostal Assemblies of the World, and offered to merge with them. (This was the same interracial group that many of these ministers had left in 1924, to form an all-white movement.)

A special joint conference was scheduled for St. Louis, November 18-20, 1931, for the purpose of consummating the merger.[14]

Before the two groups met jointly, the ministers of the Pentecostal Assemblies of the World came together to consider the offer to consolidate. They voted to empower the chairman to appoint a committee to meet representatives of the Apostolic Church of Jesus Christ, to formulate plans for amalgamation. Selected were S. N. Hancock, R. G. Pettis, G. A. White, G. B. Rowe, K. F. Smith, P. J. F. Bridges, and F. E. Curts. This list reveals that some white ministers had remained in the Pentecostal Assemblies of the World.

[12] Pentecostal Witness, May–June, 1930, p. 2.
[13] Ibid., October–November, 1931, p. 4.
[14] Pentecostal Outlook, January, 1932, p. 2.

The committee met with the one from the Apostolic Church of Jesus Christ, and, after much deliberation, returned to the assembled body with tentative conditions for merger. The entire body then passed these points upon which the merger would be based:

1. The name of the combined organizations shall be the Pentecostal Assemblies of Jesus Christ. (This name was formed by taking the first half of Pentecostal Assemblies of the World, and the last half of Apostolic Church of Jesus Christ.)

2. The Publication of the amalgamated body shall be called the Pentecostal Outlook.

3. There shall be a board of 12 to 24 presbyters, half from each race.

4. There shall be one General Secretary.

5. The Articles of Faith shall be those of the Pentecostal Assemblies of the World as they stand.

6. General headquarters shall be located in Indianapolis, Indiana.

Upon the basis of these conditions, the merger was consummated on November 18, 1931.[15]

Not everyone approved of the merger. Ministers of the former Pentecostal Assemblies of the World met in Dayton, Ohio, shortly thereafter, and voted to continue that organization.[16] Bishop Samuel K. Grimes was elected Presiding Officer, a position he held until his death thirty-five years later.

Certain white ministers of the Apostolic Church of Jesus Christ also opposed the merger, and sought to continue that organization.

But, despite all opposition, the merger was consummated, and the Pentecostal Assemblies of Jesus Christ came into being.

---

[15] Ibid.
[16] Ibid., p. 11.

7

The Pentecostal Assemblies of Jesus Christ

The latter part of chapter six told of the merging of the Apostolic Church of Jesus Christ with the Pentecostal Assemblies of the World, to form the Pentecostal Assemblies of Jesus Christ.

Ministers of both former organizations were jubilant over the merger and the new organization. Illustrative of many testimonies is this one by L. R. Ooton, first Treasurer: "I know of nothing during the past two decades that has been more blessed of God."[1]

James A. Frush, first Editor of the Pentecostal Outlook, called it one of the greatest victories over Satan, and said he believed that heaven smiled when the new organization was formed.[2] Andrew Urshan wrote a two-page article, in which he highly lauded the new movement.[3]

But there were also dissenters. Karl Smith, first Secretary of the organization, wrote of these, saying, "One of the most common utterances spoken in opposition . . . is: 'It has been tried before.' "[4] Smith meant by this that those who opposed the new interracial organization were looking back to days

---

[1] Pentecostal Outlook, August, 1932, p. 14.
[2] Ibid., February, 1932, p. 5.
[3] Ibid., August, 1932, pp. 6, 7.
[4] Ibid., p. 13.

prior to 1924, and raising the question: "If it did not work then, why should it work now?"

In spite of this opposition, well-known ministers of both races were deeply appreciative of the new movement, and were determined to make it succeed.

THE GENERAL ORGANIZATION

A Committee on Constitution had been appointed at the merger conference. This committee had recommended that the newly-formed organization accept, until its next General Assembly, the constitution and bylaws that had been used by the Pentecostal Assemblies of the World, except in those instances where they conflicted with those which would be passed at the merger conference.[5]

The General Assembly

Throughout the organization's history, this was the official name given to its annual general meeting.[6] The General Assembly was the movement's highest constitutional authority, and its primary legislative and policy making body. Actions of the official boards were brought to this body for ratification.

General Assemblies, places, and dates are listed below.

1932 – St. Louis, Missouri – August 30 – September 4
1933 – Columbus, Ohio – August 29 – September 3
1934 – Mishawaka, Indiana – September 17-23
1935 – Chicago, Illinois – September 23-29
1936 – Columbus, Ohio – September 14-20
1937 – Tulsa, Oklahoma – October 4-11
1938 – Columbus, Ohio – September 14-18
1939 – St. Paul, Minnesota – September 13-17
1940 – Pt. Arthur, Texas – September 25 – October 1
1941 – Mishawaka, Indiana – September 24-30

---

[5] Ibid., January, 1932, p. 3.
[6] Ministerial Record Book, 1945, p. 8.

1942 – St. Louis, Missouri – September 23-29
1943 – Columbus, Ohio – September 1-5
1944 – St. Louis, Missouri – September 26 – October 1
1945 – St. Louis, Missouri – September 20-26

The Board of Presbyters

It had been decided that the official General Board would consist of twenty-four Presbyters, twelve from each race.[7] However, only twelve were originally elected – six from each race.[8] Later this bylaw was changed to read: "twenty-four or less."[9] The number of Presbyters never reached twenty-four, although there were twenty-two in December, 1936. In 1945, the last year of the organization, there were sixteen. This board supervised the general work of the body.

The Executive Board

The Board of Presbyters, with the Editor of the Pentecostal Outlook, constituted the Executive Board.[10] This board took care of the organization's business between its annual general meetings.

The General Chairman

During its first seven years, the organization had no General Chairman. At each General Assembly, the Presbyter Board appointed one of its members to preside over the business meetings.

But in its seventh General Assembly, in 1938, the group voted ". . . to appoint a General Chairman to oversee and look after the general matters in our organization, the same to be chosen by and from our Board of Presbyters, serving under the direction of the board."[11]

---

[7] Pentecostal Outlook, January, 1932, p. 3.
[8] Ibid., p. 4.
[9] Ministerial Record Book, 1945, p. 8.
[10] Ibid.
[11] Pentecostal Outlook, October – November, 1938, p. 17.

The General Secretary-Treasurer

Originally, there was both a Secretary and a Treasurer. But the two offices were combined at the second General Assembly in 1933.

Manner of Election

At each General Assembly a nominating committee of three was appointed by the Chairman. This committee brought to the conference nominations for Presbyters, Secretary-Treasurer, District Elders, Editorial Staff, Missionary Board, and officials for the Pentecostal Young People's Association.

After the nominating committee had presented its list of nominees to the conference, ministers who so desired could make additional nominations from the floor.[12] There is no record that such additional nominations were ever made.

When the nominations were announced, the conference voted to ratify or reject any or all of them. The term of office was one year.

Oliver F. Fauss stated that, in effect, this method of election led to the choosing of officials by the nominating committee, since their nominations were always ratified.[13]

With little or no variation, this was the organization's method of election throughout its history.

DISTRICT ORGANIZATION

District Councils

Early in its history, the Pentecostal Assemblies of Jesus Christ passed a bylaw which read, ". . . We heartily approve the forming of district associations or councils, for the extension of the kingdom of God."[14] District Council boundaries sometimes followed those of states, but at other times parts of two states would make up one district, or several states

---

[12] Pentecostal Outlook, September, 1932, p. 23.
[13] Personal Interview.
[14] Articles of Faith, 1936, p. 11.

would be included in one District Council. The function of these districts was to supervise and carry on the work of God within their geographical boundaries.

The first District Council was formed on December 10-13, 1931, less than a month after the forming of the general organization. It was called the South Central Council, and was made up of Texas, Louisiana, Arkansas, Oklahoma, Mississippi, Tennessee, and New Mexico. There were approximately seventy-five ministers as charter members.[15] The South Central Council was to continue as an influential district throughout the organization's history.

Other councils were formed within the next few years. Of course, the movement was feeling its way, so far as district organization was concerned. Especially was this true in areas where its constituency was so sparse that districts had to include parts of more than one state. Councils were formed, and re-formed, to create the best working relationship.

Some of the District Councils were: Illinois, Southern Missouri – Northern Arkansas, California, Indiana, Wisconsin, Northern District, Southern District, Northwestern and Central States, Mississippi, Colorado, South Carolina, Pacific-Southwest, New Jersey, Western Pennsylvania, Idaho, Eastern, and Southeastern.

District Elders

Bylaws of the Pentecostal Assemblies of Jesus Christ called for ". . . a board of District Elders, sufficient in number to meet the need of the body." [16] They, too, were elected at the General Assembly, for a one-year term.

District Elders were to oversee the work in the "field of their location." They were to work in conjunction with local pastors and assemblies, whenever called upon by these pastors or assemblies.[17]

---

[15] Pentecostal Outlook, January, 1932, p. 11.
[16] Ministerial Record Book, 1945, p. 8.
[17] Ibid., p. 10.

District Elders were "area" men. It was not necessarily the case that a District Elder was the sole supervisor of the District Council in which he lived. Residing within the boundaries of certain districts were two, are even three, District Elders.

Organized States

When a District Council embraced more than one state, sometimes each state within the district would also be organized. An example of this was Texas and Louisiana, both within the South Central Council. These states held separate conventions, camp meetings, etc.

State Chairmen were elected within those states over which they had supervision. Their main function was to preside over state conventions. Some District Elders were also State Chairmen, performing their council duties, and also supervising the work of an organized state.

LOCAL CHURCHES

The Pentecostal Assemblies of Jesus Christ had a brief form of local church government, consisting of six statements, for those churches affiliated with the organization. Four of the six statements pertained to church property, and one concerned the obtaining of a letter of recommendation when changing churches.[18]

GENERAL OFFICIALS

As already stated, seven years passed before the Pentecostal Assemblies of Jesus Christ elected a General Chairman. In 1938 W. T. Witherspoon was chosen to fill this position, and continued in office until 1945, when the group merged with the Pentecostal Church, Incorporated.

The first Secretary was Karl F. Smith; the first Treasurer, L. R. Ooton. The two offices were soon combined, and Smith

---

[18] Ibid., p. 14.

served as Secretary-Treasurer until 1936. That year, at the General Assembly in Tulsa, Oklahoma, James A. Frush was elected to replace Smith. Frush held the office until 1938, when he resigned, due to poor health, and the pressure of pastoral duties. Stanley R. Hanby reluctantly accepted the position, and held it until 1945.

Departmental officials will be listed under DEPARTMENTAL ORGANIZATION.

MINISTERIAL MEMBERSHIP

Membership Requirements

To hold a license or credential with the Pentecostal Assemblies of Jesus Christ, one had to be at least twenty-one years of age.

He must have received the baptism of the Holy Ghost, have been baptized in Jesus' name, and believe in and preach the same. He must have had the baptism of the Holy Ghost for at least two years. An exception was made in the case of ministers who had previously been ordained in other accredited organizations, and who were otherwise qualified to hold full credentials.

A candidate for admission must have worked in some local assembly for at least one year, and must have a letter of recommendation from the pastor.

At the time of making application, the candidate for admission had to be examined by three elders—a Presbyter, a District Elder, and a pastor. If found qualified, he was granted a license or credential, upon presenting his letter of recommendation to the General Secretary. A new credential or license was issued annually.[19]

Membership for Women Ministers

Credentials given to women ministers were to read, "Missionary," or "Evangelist."[20]

[19] Ibid., p. 12.
[20] Ibid., p. 11.

They were permitted to perform weddings, conduct funerals, baptize candidates, and serve Communion ". . . in case of emergency."

A woman minister could take charge of an assembly only until a man was raised up in the church, qualified in every way to assume leadership. This was true, even though this woman minister had started the work.[21]

DEPARTMENTAL ORGANIZATION

Elaborate departmental organization came relatively late in Oneness Pentecostal movements. In the beginning, there was little need for such organization.

Foreign Missionary Department

The Pentecostal Assemblies of Jesus Christ was interested in foreign missions from the beginning.

The organization formulated a nine-point foreign missionary policy which dealt with the handling of foreign missionary funds, requirements for missionaries before going to the field, the purchase of property on the field, missionary furloughs, etc.

It was recommended that the first Sunday of each month be set aside as foreign missionary Sunday, and that a special offering for foreign missions be taken on that Sunday.[22]

W. T. Witherspoon became the first Missionary Chairman. He said, ". . . the policy of this department has not been to discriminate against missionaries who may belong to other Oneness organizations; in fact, in more than one case we have advised missionaries to take out papers with other organizations, as well as ours. First of all, because we have no right to insist that a missionary belong only to the Pentecostal Assemblies of Jesus Christ, since we are not in a position to fully support any station."[23]

[21] Ibid., p. 9.
[22] Articles of Faith, 1936, pp. 13, 14.
[23] Pentecostal Outlook, July, 1933, p. 11.

This policy was carried out, for, in checking those missionaries partially supported, one finds several who also received funds from the Pentecostal Church, Incorporated.

Missionaries supported through the years were: *China* — Elizabeth Steiglitz, Ralph Bullock, Mabel Hensley, Mae Iry; *India* — Joseph Rezniczek, Mrs. D. L. McCarty, H. O. Tefre, James Morar; *Africa* — L. Badger, Mrs. C. A. Tucker, A. J. and Pearl Holmes; *Japan* — L. W. Coote, R. A. Fleming; *Jerusalem* — Timothy Urshan; *Iraq* — J. B. Thomas; *South America* — L. B. Sly, J. Elmer Bell; *Hawaii* — E. D. Stiles; and *Czechoslovakia* — John Huba.

Foreign missionary offerings for 1933–1934, the first years for which we have available records, were $7,320.96. The amount increased little until during the more prosperous years of World War II, and then it rose rapidly. For the twelve-month period ending August, 1945, the offerings totaled $23,705.14.

Witherspoon continued as Missionary Chairman until 1944, when he was succeeded by Wynn T. Stairs.[24]

Youth Department

The Pentecostal Assemblies of Jesus Christ had youth groups in its local churches, and district youth organizations, before there was an actively functioning national youth work.

At its second General Assembly, the organization passed the following: "Resolved, That we create a National Young People's Association, consisting of all young people's associations in the general body, and that the second day of the General Assembly be devoted to this association." [25] Note: The first day was usually used instead of the second.

The PYPA was organized in 1934, at the third General Assembly, under the direction of Mary Williams. Officers were a President, a Vice President, and a Secretary-Treasurer.[26]

[24] Ibid., November, 1944, p. 2.
[25] Ibid., September, 1933, p. 22.
[26] Ibid., October, 1934, p. 20.

It was required that the President be an ordained minister. In the beginning, his main duty was to preside at national youth meetings.

A membership certificate was issued to each youth group.[27]

The constitution for the PYPA, consisting of six articles, was published for the first time in the 1936 Articles of Faith, on pages 15 and 16.

Brady Robinson was the first President. He was succeeded in 1938 by Wallace McKeehan, who served until 1940, when Arthur Witherspoon was elected. In 1943 Eldredge Lewis was chosen President, and served until the merger in 1945. (He died suddenly in an explosion on December 5, 1946.)

The first national PYPA convention, apart from the General Assembly, was held in Tulsa, Oklahoma, March 28-31, 1942.[28] Another national convention was also held in Tulsa in May, 1945. Young people from twelve states attended.[29]

Sunday School Department

The Pentecostal Assemblies of Jesus Christ had no national Sunday school Department, although there were district Sunday school organizations which held conventions, and functioned otherwise on a district level.

DOCTRINAL POSITION

When the Apostolic Church of Jesus Christ merged with the Pentecostal Assemblies of the World, to form the Pentecostal Assemblies of Jesus Christ, there was no doctrinal change, as both groups were doctrinally identical.

As all other Oneness organizations, the movement believed in repentance; water baptism in the name of the Lord Jesus Christ; and the receiving of the Holy Ghost, with the

---

[27] Ministerial Record Book, 1945, p. 16.
[28] Pentecostal Outlook, May, 1942, p. 19.
[29] Ibid., June, 1945, p. 11.

initial sign of speaking with other tongues (languages) as the Spirit gave utterance.[30]

Most of the ministers in the organization believed that water baptism in Jesus' name remitted sins, and was the same as being born of water.[31] They further believed that the receiving of the baptism of the Holy Ghost was synonymous with being born of the Spirit.[32]

Ministers in the group also believed that one could, and did, receive a spiritual experience before being filled with the Holy Ghost. This they usually called conversion.

W. T. Witherspoon turned to God in a Methodist Episcopal Church in 1901, but did not receive the Holy Ghost until 1912.[33] Oliver Fauss turned to the Lord in a Nazarene Church in 1910, and received the Holy Ghost in 1911.[34] James A. Frush said, "I was brought up in a Methodist Church, and was converted at the age of 16. . . ." He received the Holy Ghost much later, in 1915.[35]

In recounting his experience, W. C. Chapman said, "In 1915 I began attending the Southern Methodist Church. Being deeply under conviction (in a revival) I went to the altar and poured out my heart unto God for several hours. The burden of sin rolled off my soul, and I praised God in loud tones. I lived for Christ in all the light I had. . . ."[36] He received the Holy Ghost in 1919.

PUBLICATIONS

Publishing House

The Pentecostal Assemblies of Jesus Christ, as a national organization, never owned a publishing house.

[30] Acts 2:4, 38.
[31] John 3:5.
[32] Ibid.
[33] Pentecostal Outlook, December, 1938, p. 2.
[34] Ibid., March, 1939, p. 2.
[35] Ibid., May, 1939, p. 2.
[36] Ibid., April, 1940, p. 2.

The South Central Council, one of its larger districts, organized a publishing house in August, 1935. Located at Kilgore, Texas, it was known as the South Central Council Publishing House. This publishing house did much of the printing for the entire organization. (See under Sunday School Literature.)

The Pentecostal Outlook

This monthly periodical was the official voice of the organization. Its name came from the first half of the Pentecostal Witness, and the last half of the Christian Outlook, official organs of the two groups which merged to form the Pentecostal Assemblies of Jesus Christ in 1931.

The first Editor was James A. Frush. Associate Editors were S. K. Grimes and O. F. Fauss. When Frush became Editor, the place of publication was moved from Indianapolis, Indiana to Newark, Ohio, where it remained during his tenure of office.

When Frush resigned in September, 1938, due to failing health and the burden of pastoral duties, he was succeeded by S. G. Norris of St. Paul, Minnesota, and the place of publication was moved to that city.

First published as a sixteen-page periodical, the paper was soon increased to twenty-eight pages. During 1939, the page size was increased, and the number of pages decreased to twenty. This was the size of the periodical throughout the remainder of the organization's history.

Sunday School Literature

The publishing of Sunday school literature was first mentioned at the second General Assembly in 1933, when the organization passed the rather unusual resolution "That a committee of three be appointed to approach all other Oneness organizations to consummate a Sunday School Department, composed of chosen members of all Oneness organizations, to the intent that they may be a party to the formulating, editing, and using Oneness Sunday school literature, which the department shall supply. . . ."[37]

Put simply, this resolution called for the different Oneness organizations to cooperate in the publishing of Sunday school literature. The Pentecostal Assemblies of Jesus Christ saw the need for Oneness Pentecostal literature, but did not feel able to produce it alone. The plan had its good points. It is doubtful, however, that the Pentecostal Church, Incorporated would have gone along, as they had been publishing their own Sunday school literature since April of 1930.

The aforementioned committee made a report at the 1934 General Assembly, but apparently nothing further was done.

The South Central Council, in its 1935 meeting, took it upon itself to begin working toward the publishing of Sunday school literature. Every church in the council was asked to begin raising money for the project.[38] T. F. Ford, South Central Council Sunday School Superintendent, was in charge of the endeavor.

The South Central Council began publishing literature for the first quarter of 1937, at Kilgore, Texas. They printed a Junior, an Intermediate, and an Adult quarterly. This Sunday school literature was published for the entire organization.[39]

Later, T. F. Ford wrote, ". . . the volume of business has grown to such an extent that we feel the time is ripe to install our own printing machinery. . . ."[40]

HEADQUARTERS

The first headquarters of the Pentecostal Assemblies of Jesus Christ was in Indianapolis, Indiana, which had also been the headquarters city of the Pentecostal Assemblies of the World.

[37] Ibid., September, 1933, p. 22.
[38] Ibid., March, 1936, p. 24.
[39] Ibid., December, 1936, p. 26.
[40] Ibid., July, 1938, p. 21.

In an official board meeting, held at Columbus, Ohio, March 22, 1932, it was decided to move the headquarters to Columbus. This decision was apparently due to opposition from those of the Pentecostal Assemblies of the World who had continued the organization after the majority of its members had merged with the Apostolic Church of Jesus Christ.[41]

The Pentecostal Assemblies of Jesus Christ did not have a centralized headquarters for all its departments. In 1945, its last year, the office of the General Chairman was in Columbus, Ohio, while the Secretary-Treasurer's office was at Lancaster, Ohio. All matters concerning the Pentecostal Outlook were addressed to St. Paul, Minnesota. Sunday school correspondence went to Kilgore, Texas. The office of the Foreign Missionary Department was located in West Tulsa, Oklahoma.

CHRISTIAN EDUCATION

The Pentecostal Assemblies of Jesus Christ endorsed three Bible schools.

Apostolic Bible Institute

This school, the first for the organization, was founded by S. G. Norris in St. Paul, Minnesota. It began its first term on October 4, 1937, with fourteen students from eight states. Courses taught were Old Testament, New Testament, Church History, English, Public Speaking, and Ministerial Problems.[42] The school has been highly successful, and has grown throughout the years. In 1944 there were 80 students.

Note: As this school continued after the forming of the United Pentecostal Church, its history will be taken up in chapter eleven.

Apostolic College

First known as Apostolic Bible Training School, this institution was begun in 1938 at Tulsa, Oklahoma by C. P. and

[41] Ibid., April, 1932, p. 12.
[42] Ibid., 1937, pp. 14, 15.

Mary Williams. At first it was only a mid-winter school. But in 1939 it opened on October 2, and continued until March 30, 1940. The school offered courses in Bible, Church History, Instrumental and Vocal Music, Secretarial Work, English, Printing, etc.[43] There were ninety-four students enrolled for the 1944 term.[44]

Southern Bible and Vocational College

This school had its beginning at Rising Star, Texas in 1939. In 1943 it moved to Milford, Texas. In charge was L. C. Reed. It advertised to teach all elementary and high school grades, as well as vocational and business courses. It also offered Bible teaching, and courses in more advanced literary subjects.[45] The school continued through 1944.

INTERRACIAL RELATIONSHIP

In chapter three it was noted that many white ministers of the Pentecostal Assemblies of the World felt it best to leave the interracial organization, and form an all-white movement. This occurred in 1924. A few white ministers remained with the Pentecostal Assemblies of the World.

Then, as stated later, the Apostolic Church of Jesus Christ merged with the Pentecostal Assemblies of the World in 1931, to form the Pentecostal Assemblies of Jesus Christ (chapter six).

The first part of this present chapter told how ministers of both races rejoiced over the new organization.

But it was not long until the group encountered the same difficulties that had hindered the earlier interracial alliance. The main problem grew out of the strict segregation laws in the South. Negro ministers from the North could not find suitable accommodations in the South, hence four out of the first five General Assemblies were held in the North.

[43] Ibid., September, 1939, p. 20.
[44] Ibid., July, 1945, p. 12.
[45] Ibid., December, 1943, p. 14.

As early as December, 1931, within one month after the merger, the newly-formed South Central Council, made up of states in the deep South, sent this request to the General Presbyter Board: "Resolved, That we ask the Honorable Board of Bishops to place the General Assembly as far south as possible. We request that St. Louis, Missouri be chosen." [46] From this request, it seems that St. Louis was as far south as these brethren felt the general convention could be taken, and still have fair representation.

In those days, much of the country was still in the grip of the depression. In general, Pentecostal ministers were not as affluent as they are today. Because of this, not many from the South could attend the General Assemblies. The following statement bears this out: "All of our conferences heretofore have been held in the North, and . . . there are hundreds of our dear brethren who cannot possibly attend our conferences in the North. . . ." [47]

Finally, the ministers saw that something must be done. Consequently, in their fifth General Assembly in 1936 they passed the following: "Be it resolved, That, in fairness to many who have been hindered from attending General Assemblies, which are restricted to Northern states, we henceforth endorse taking the conventions anywhere in the United States the body desires." [48]

In that same meeting they also voted that the personnel of the Presbyter Board should be determined according to the percentage of ministerial membership of the two races, which, they said, was then about 80% white and 20% colored.[49] Before this, the board had consisted of an equal number of ministers from each race.

Finally, this was passed: "Since the General Secretary-Treasurer for about five years has been colored, Be it Re-

[46] Ibid., January, 1932, p. 11.
[47] Ibid., April, 1937, p. 20.
[48] Ibid., October, 1936, p. 18.
[49] Ibid.

solved, That we make a choice of a white Secretary-Treasurer." [50]

One gathers, from these three resolutions, that a different attitude had developed. There was no racial prejudice, but a majority of the ministers felt that the organization had gone too far in helping one segment of its constituency, at the expense of another. Now this was to be changed.

In accordance with the resolution to take the General Assembly anywhere in the United States, the 1937 meeting was held in Tulsa, Oklahoma. Glowing testimonies were given of this meeting. Perhaps the presence of many Southern ministers who had never attended a general convention had something to do with the blessed spirit of the gathering.

Few, if any, Negro ministers were present in the Tulsa meeting. For that reason, little business was transacted, and what was done was to be ratified at the 1938 General Assembly, to be held in Columbus, Ohio.

At the Columbus meeting certain Negro officials resigned, and returned to the Pentecostal Assemblies of the World. For the first time in its history, the Pentecostal Assemblies of Jesus Christ had an all-white Presbyter Board.[51]

GROWTH

The ministerial list for 1936 showed 981 ministers. The list for 1945, the last year of the organization, showed 1,028, an increase of only 47. But this slow growth was caused by many Negro ministers' leaving the organization between 1938 and 1945, to return to the Pentecostal Assemblies of the World.

The 1945 ministerial record showed 324 churches. But according to Stanley R. Hanby, General Secretary, this list did not include many of their churches.

This group soon merged with the Pentecostal Church, Incorporated, to form the United Pentecostal Church.

---

[50] Ibid.
[51] Ibid., December, 1938, p. 19.

8

The Pentecostal Church, Incorporated

The Pentecostal Ministerial Alliance changed its name to Pentecostal Church, Incorporated in October, 1932, but it was not until February, 1933 that the change of name was published, due to the desire of the officials to be sure the new name had not already been chartered by some other group. When they found it had not, the name was carried through the court, and the change became official.[1]

Reason for the Change

W. E. Kidson said, "The object of this change is that we might have a name which embodies the meaning that churches could be or are affiliated with us, since it is not our desire to be strictly a ministerial organization, but rather do all that we can in assisting and protecting God's people. Nearly everyone has been quite anxious that we adopt a name which can be used universally in connection with our churches. . . .

"We are living in serious times, therefore we need protection for the laity, and it was with this thought in mind that the brethren unanimously decided to change the name."[2]

Of course, other organizations were also incorporated under their official names, but they did not feature the word *incorporated* as prominently as did this group. The new movement did so, apparently, because there were so many Pente-

---

[1] Apostolic Herald, February, 1933, p. 4.
[2] Ibid.

costal churches, and they wanted everyone to know that their name was legally theirs alone.

THE GENERAL ORGANIZATION

In the beginning, as could be expected, the general organizational structure of the Pentecostal Church, Incorporated was identical with that of the Pentecostal Ministerial Alliance. But gradually, through the years, changes occurred in governmental structure and procedure.

The General Conference

As in all Oneness organizations, the annual general meeting of the Pentecostal Church, Incorporated was its foremost authority. The organization called this meeting the General Conference, since this was the name adopted earlier by the Pentecostal Ministerial Alliance.

In the General Conference, departmental reports were read, general officials were elected, appointments were presented for ratification, actions of official boards were considered, and resolutions were discussed and voted upon.

Places and dates of General Conferences are given below. The first meeting listed is really the ninth annual General Conference of the organization.

1933 – Louisiana, Missouri – October 17 – 26
1934 – Dallas, Texas – October 23 – November 1
1935 – Jackson, Tennessee – October 18 – 24
1936 – St. Louis, Missouri – October 22 – 28
1937 – Jackson, Tennessee – October 22 – 28
1938 – Houston, Texas – October 14 – 20
1939 – East St. Louis, Illinois – Aug. 28 – Sept. 6
1940 – Jackson, Tennessee – October 24 – 30
1941 – Houston, Texas – October 31 – November 6
1942 – Memphis, Tennessee – November 5 – 13
1943 – Hot Springs, Arkansas – November 4 – 10
1944 – Jonesboro, Arkansas – October 24 – 31
1945 – St. Louis, Missouri – September 20 – 26

General Conference of the Pentecostal Church, Incorporated, Houston, Texas, October 14 to 20, 1938.

Board of General Presbyters

Originally, there were seven General Presbyters. Later, when the District Presbyter over each district automatically became a General Presbyter, and a member of the General Board, the number increased to nine.

Until 1941, General Presbyters were elected for a term of one year. At that time, the term of office was extended to two years.

The duties of the General Presbyters were to "... work for the welfare of the entire organization."[3] They normally met at each General Conference, three days prior to the beginning of the meeting. Special sessions could be called at any time, if the occasion demanded.

In the earlier days of the movement, the General Presbyter served as Chairman of the District Board in the district of which he was overseer.[4]

For a time in the organization's history, the Board of General Presbyters was given rather broad powers. In 1936 this resolution was passed: "When deemed necessary, the General Board shall have the right to adopt or annul any bylaw, and the same shall be operative until the following General Conference, when it shall be considered as any other business."[5]

The Executive Board

This board was made up of different officials at various times in the organization's history. At first it was composed of the General Chairman, General Secretary, and General Missionary Secretary. Later the General Sunday School Superintendent replaced the Missionary Secretary. And, for a time, this board was made up of the aforementioned four officials, plus three other members.[6] In its final form, the Executive

---

[3] Minutes, 8th General Conference, p. 44.
[4] Discipline of Pentecostal Church, Incorporated, p. 13.
[5] Apostolic Herald, November, 1936, p. 6.
[6] Minutes of 13th General Conference, p. 82.

Board members were, as in the beginning, the General Superintendent, the General Secretary, and the General Missionary Secretary.[7]

The Executive Board took care of the organization's general business between General Board meetings. It represented the entire organization, and had no jurisdiction over any certain district.[8]

In 1939 this board was granted powers similar to those given earlier to the General Board, by this resolution: "... any change made by the Executive Board in the bylaws, as set forth in the Discipline, must be published in the Herald at least once before it becomes effective.[9] There is no record that this authority was ever used.

The General Chairman

The Pentecostal Church, Incorporated began its history without a General Chairman. Howard Goss had resigned as General Superintendent of the Pentecostal Ministerial Alliance in March, 1932. In the General Conference that year the group voted to abolish the office.

But in 1934, at the tenth General Conference, the organization voted to elect a General Chairman. It was further requested that the chairman devote as much time as possible to the work, and that he serve without a stipulated salary.[10] He was not asked to give full time to the work of the organization.

In 1939, at the fifteenth General Conference, the name General Chairman was changed to General Superintendent. In that same meeting it was decided that the General Superintendent should go on the field as a full-time official.[11] This

---

[7] Apostolic Herald, October, 1945, p. 2.
[8] Minutes of 13th General Conference, p. 82.
[9] Minutes of 15th General Conference, p. 90.
[10] Apostolic Herald, November, 1934, p. 5.
[11] Ibid., September, 1939, p. 3.

was the first time any Oneness organization had taken such a forward step.

The General Secretary-Treasurer

Originally, the function of the General Secretary was to take minutes, and preserve records of business proceedings, with all other papers belonging to the organization.

But during the time that the organization had no General Chairman, the Secretary took over certain responsibilities of this office. He directed the business of the Headquarters Office, called General and Executive Board meetings, and presided over them.[12]

These duties were, of course, relinquished when the group again elected a General Chairman.

Manner of Election

At first, general officials were nominated by a nominating committee of three (bylaws called for a committee of from three to five) at General Conference, and were then voted upon by the assembled ministers and delegates. All ministers and delegates had the right to suggest nominees to this committee.[13]

The nominating committee brought to the conference only one name for each office. The assembled ministers and delegates voted either to accept or reject the nominations. (There is no record that any nomination was ever rejected.)

The General Board of Presbyters nominated the members of the Foreign Missionary Board, members of the Board of Publication, and the Editor of the Apostolic Herald. These, too, were voted upon by the General Conference.[14]

A change was made in the nominating procedure in 1937 at the General Conference. The nominating committee then brought to the conference the names of three whom they considered best for each office, and the conference was allowed to

---

[12] Discipline of Pentecostal Church, Incorporated, p. 11.
[13] Ibid.
[14] Apostolic Herald, November, 1936, p. 5.

vote on which of the three they desired. Nominations were made one day prior to election day.[15] Thus the members of the organization were given a greater voice in the selection of their general officials.

It was not until 1943, however, that the General Conference was allowed to both nominate and elect its officials. This resolution was then passed: "The first ballot shall be a nominating ballot, and the names of the three receiving the highest number of votes (for each office) shall be presented to the conference to be voted upon for election." [16] This did away with the nominating committee.

DISTRICT ORGANIZATION

Formation of Districts

As the Pentecostal Church, Incorporated began organizing its work upon a district level, it encountered the same problems that other Oneness groups had faced. Not the least of these was the determining of geographical boundaries best suited for the work.

This difficulty led to the forming, and then re-forming, of some districts. For instance, the Illinois District and the Missouri District merged to form (along with other states) the Central District. Later, however, Missouri withdrew and formed a district of its own. There were several other changes.

In the last year of the organization's history there were nine districts: East Central, Central, Missouri, Southeastern, Southwestern, South-Central, Texico, Western, and Northwestern.

District Presbyters

In 1932, the Pentecostal Church, Incorporated adopted a detailed plan for district organization. A District Presbyter, elected in the district, was to be District Chairman, presiding

[15] Ibid., November, 1937, p. 4.
[16] Minutes, 19th General Conference, p. 111.

over all district meetings. But the General Presbyter of the district, who was still elected at General Conference, was to preside over District Board meetings.[17]

At the General Conference in 1936 a resolution was passed ". . . that the offices of General and District Presbyters be combined, and that the District Presbyter of each district elected this year in the districts automatically become a General Presbyter at General Conference."[18] This did away with the electing of General Presbyters at the General Conference, and also eliminated what was certainly an overlapping of duties in the districts.

This procedure of choosing General Presbyters was later adopted by the United Pentecostal Church.

LOCAL CHURCHES

Any local assembly could be affiliated with, and under the protection of, the Pentecostal Church, Incorporated by adopting the fundamentals, bylaws, and the form of local church government passed at the 1932 General Conference.[19]

This comprehensive form of local church government was rather a marvel in completeness for those days. It covered pages 47 to 52 in the typewritten minutes of the conference. It dealt with eligibility of members, the manner of admission, duties and obligations of members, church discipline, officers and their duties, the holding of property, etc.

GENERAL OFFICIALS

In 1934, two years after its beginning, the Pentecostal Church, Incorporated elected B. H. Hite, well-known minister of St. Louis, as its first General Chairman. Hite continued in office until 1939, when Howard A. Goss was elected as full-time General Superintendent. Goss left his pastorate in Toronto,

---

[17] Ibid., 8th General Conference, p. 54.
[18] Apostolic Herald, November, 1936, p. 16.
[19] Minutes, 8th General Conference, p. 45.

Canada, and returned to the States to assume his duties. He served throughout the remainder of the organization's history.

W. E. Kidson, who had been elected General Secretary of the Pentecostal Ministerial Alliance in 1928, was retained in office when the organization became the Pentecostal Church, Incorporated. He served until 1943, when Harry Branding, another well-known St. Louis minister, was elected. After only eight months in office, Branding resigned, and Oscar Vouga was appointed by the General Board to fill his unexpired term. Vouga continued in office until the 1945 General Conference.

MINISTERIAL MEMBERSHIP

The basic requirement for membership in the Pentecostal Church, Incorporated was plainly set forth in this bylaw: "To be affiliated with this organization, one must have had the one baptism of the Holy Ghost, with the initial sign of speaking in other tongues, as in Acts 2:4; 10:46; 19:1-6; have been baptized by immersion in the name of the Lord Jesus Christ, as in Acts 2:38; and believe in, teach, and preach the same."[20]

A questionnaire was to be properly filled out, and endorsed by a District Presbyter or District Secretary.[21]

After preaching one sermon per week for six months, and being passed by the District Board, a minister was granted a Local License. Then, after preaching for one year, a General License was granted.[22]

No minister was ordained until he had held a General License, had been in the active ministry as a pastor or an evangelist for two full consecutive years, and had been fully proven.[23]

DEPARTMENTAL ORGANIZATION

The Pentecostal Church, Incorporated organized only

[20] Discipline of Pentecostal Church, Incorporated, p. 25.
[21] Ibid.
[22] Minutes of 19th General Conference, p. 112.
[23] Discipline of Pentecostal Church, Incorporated, p. 26.

three departments on a national scale. The first of these was the

Foreign Missionary Department

Two things reveal that they considered foreign missions extremely important: (1) The Foreign Missionary Department was the first one organized, and (2) the Foreign Missionary Secretary (actually, the chairman) was a member of the Executive Board through most of the organization's history.

Clarence Craine was elected Foreign Missionary Secretary in 1933. He was followed by Harry Morse in 1935. Morse resigned in 1938, and A. O. Moore (formerly a missionary to India) was elected. Moore held the office until 1945.

Missionary offerings in 1933 were only $1,651.73; in 1935, $4,612.02; but in 1940 they increased to $10,056.10.

Missionaries supported wholly or partially through the years were: *China* — Mae Iry, Elsie King, Ralph and Lona May Bullock, Dan and Alice Sheets, Garland and Eleanor Leonard (Garland Leonard was martyred by the Chinese in 1937), Henry and Gladys McCune; *India* — Henry and Olive Tefre, Dorothy L. McCarty, L. E. Haney, Jeanette Wright, Henrietta Wise, Joseph and Faith Rezniczek; *West Africa* — A. J. and Pearl Holmes, Otis M. Petty, Peter Jensen; *Java* — George and Helen White; *Japan* — Joseph Murata; and *Palestine* — Louise Dickson.

In 1941 the organization voted to return 25% of all undesignated foreign missionary funds to the district from which they came, to be used in opening new works.[24] This was, in a sense, the beginning of organized home missions.

The movement adopted a comprehensive foreign missionary policy in 1944, setting forth qualifications for prospective missionaries, and rules applicable to missionary conduct, financial support, etc.

---

[24] Minutes, 17th General Conference, p. 103.

Sunday School Department

W. E. Kidson said, "In the beginning of the latter rain out-pouring, many were skeptical, or at least dilatory, about Sunday school. After losing quite a number of young folk and children, we began to realize that we were making a mistake...."[25]

Dan Hayes was elected General Sunday School Superintendent in 1932. He was intensely active in this work throughout the movement. He held this office until the General Conference of 1941.

In that conference, the organization passed a resolution: "... that the National Sunday School Department be abolished, and that we recommend that each district organize its own work."[26]

Apparently the group felt that, on a national scale, the Sunday school work had shown unsatisfactory progress.

A committee was appointed in the 1944 General Conference to seek to reorganize the Sunday school work on a national basis,[27] but before this was brought about, the group merged with the Pentecostal Assemblies of Jesus Christ.

Youth Department

In 1930 the young people's group of the Pentecostal Ministerial Alliance had adopted the name Pentecostal Gleaners, and this name was carried over into the Pentecostal Church, Incorporated.

The avowed purpose of the Gleaners was to promote spirituality among young people already saved, and to carry the gospel to young people who were lost.[28]

Dan Hayes was elected Gleaners President in 1933. He served until 1943, when T. Richard Reed was elected. In 1937 Reed was succeeded by J. L. Newgent, who held the office until 1941.

[25] Apostolic Herald, March, 1941, p. 16.
[26] Minutes, 17th General Conference, p. 100.
[27] Apostolic Herald, December, 1944, p. 14.
[28] Ibid., January, 1933, p. 3.

The Gleaners were usually given one day at the General Conference. Other than this, they had no national meetings.

In the 1941 General Conference the National Gleaners Organization was abolished, and it was recommended that each district organize its own work.[29]

As in the case of the Sunday School Department, a committee was appointed in 1944 to reorganize the national youth department, but this was never carried out. However, the youth work continued to grow on the local and district level.

DOCTRINAL POSITION

The doctrinal position of the Pentecostal Church, Incorporated was identical with that of the Pentecostal Ministerial Alliance. (This organization's belief concerning the plan of salvation is set forth in chapter four, page 47.) And for a further explanation of what the Pentecostal Church, Incorporated believed relative to the plan of salvation, see chapter ten, page 120.

Basically, the organization believed that this plan is found in Acts 2:4, 38. These verses speak of repentance, water baptism in the name of Jesus for the remission of sins, and the receiving of the Holy Ghost, evidenced by speaking with other tongues.

Concerning water baptism in Jesus' name, Howard Goss, General Superintendent, wrote: "Some interpret water baptism as a means of getting sins remitted, but Peter said, 'for' (in Acts 2:38), which, as used here, means because your sins have been remitted."[30]

There were others in the organization who did not agree with Goss' interpretation concerning water baptism, believing that this ordinance did remit sins.

To make it plainer, some believed that one's sins were remitted by virtue of the efficacy of Jesus' shed blood, and that

---

[29] Minutes, 17th General Conference, p. 100.
[30] Apostolic Herald, June, 1941, p. 3.

this remission occurred when the sinner genuinely repented. But others in the organization believed just as strongly that this was effected by water baptism in Jesus' name, which was the same as being born of water.[31]

Similarly, some in the Pentecostal Church, Incorporated believed that one was saved, and then received the baptism of the Holy Ghost. Others strongly affirmed that one was not saved, or born again, until he had received the baptism of the Spirit.

In view of all this, one cannot say that the organization, as a whole, believed either way. To do so is to assume that the few leaders, in speaking or writing, expressed the beliefs of the entire constituency, and this was not the case. Hundreds of "grass roots" ministers had no opportunity to express their beliefs in such a way as to be recorded for posterity.

Finally, let it be remembered that the Pentecostal Church, Incorporated, as had the Pentecostal Ministerial Alliance before it, granted considerable latitude concerning the doctrine of the new birth. This was the basis upon which the organization had been founded.

PUBLICATIONS

The Herald Publishing House

This name grew out of the fact that, in the beginning, the organization published nothing but the Apostolic Herald.

In 1935 the movement voted to sell its publishing house to W. E. Kidson, then General Secretary. Apparently this was done because of some difficulty which arose relative to the conducting of the business. The organization agreed to endorse the Sunday school literature published by the Herald Publishing House, so long as it was doctrinally correct, and further agreed to refrain from publishing or recommending any other. If the group decided it wanted a publishing house at some later

---

[31] John 3:5.

date, it would buy the Herald Publishing House back from Kidson, at the current market price, or give him six months notice before beginning another.[32]

It was not until 1942 that the organization took steps to again have its own publishing house. Ethel Goss said, "It was enthusiastically voted by the General Conference to buy a publishing house, . . . and $4,500 was pledged for that purpose." [33]

The question was: Where should they buy? At a meeting of the Executive Board in January, 1944, it was decided not to purchase the Herald Publishing House from W. E. Kidson, as it had been the opinion of the conference that the facility should be located more centrally.

Of course, the location of the publishing house would soon be settled, with the purchase of property in St. Louis.

The Apostolic Herald

Throughout its history, the Pentecostal Church, Incorporated published the Apostolic Herald, its official voice, each month.

W. E. Kidson was Editor from 1932 until 1935, when A. D. Gurley was appointed to the position. Gurley resigned in May, 1937, due to poor health, and the responsibility of pastoring two churches. Sam McClain became Editor in November, 1937, but did not move to headquarters until 1939. He continued to serve until 1941, though he had accepted a church in Rupert, Idaho in June, 1940.

Kidson, who had been Managing Editor through the years, now became Editor.

In January, 1943, A. D. Hunter, formerly General Secretary of the Pentecostal Church of God, was appointed Editor. At the General Conference in November, 1943, Hunter stated that he did not wish to continue as Editor, and Oscar Vouga was appointed. He held this position through 1945.

---

[32] Apostolic Herald, November, 1935, p. 9.
[33] Ibid., December, 1942, p. 14.

No figures are available to show the growth of the paper, but its circulation increased steadily through the years.

Sunday School Literature

As stated in chapter four, the Pentecostal Ministerial Alliance began publishing Sunday school literature in the second quarter of 1930.

From the year of 1934, the Pentecostal Church, Incorporated talked of purchasing printing equipment, and printing its own Sunday school literature. But it was not until much later that this became a reality. In July, 1937, W. E. Kidson said, "Several months ago our dream started to come true. We are now printing . . . a part of our Sunday school literature, and within the next thirty days we hope to be printing . . . all our own literature."[34]

According to reports, the sale of the literature climbed steadily through the years.

HEADQUARTERS

One wonders if the Pentecostal Church, Incorporated did not establish some kind of record in moving its headquarters from city to city.

The first headquarters city was Louisiana, Missouri. There, in 1933, the group purchased a large, forty-five bedroom hotel, planning to enlarge the dining room, and convert it into an auditorium. This was the first property owned by the organization.

In July, 1934, headquarters was moved to Dallas, Texas. Said Kidson, "We have realized for quite a number of years that we would have a greater opportunity in a larger city . . . None appealed to us as strongly as Dallas." There the group purchased a large, old Jewish mansion. But in May, 1935, they moved to another location in the city.

---

[34] Ibid., July, 1937, p. 4.

The headquarters was moved from Dallas to Houston in June, 1939.

Apparently the organization was growing somewhat weary of all this moving. In late 1939 it considered buying property in East St. Louis, Illinois for a permanent headquarters. B. H. Hite had made the down payment on a former orphanage, located at 5701 Belmont Avenue. But at its General Conference the group decided not to purchase the property, and reimbursed Hite for what he had paid.[35]

In that same conference it was also decided to leave the headquarters in Houston.

The decision to build a headquarters building was made in a General Board meeting, held in Houston, May 6, 1941. Property was purchased, and a building erected at 1320 North 67th Street, in Houston. The building was of wood, ninety feet long and thirty-eight feet wide. It was adequate then, but by today's standards it would seem pitifully small.

Headquarters of the organization remained in Houston until 1944. Then, in compliance with a resolution passed at the 1943 General Conference, the General Board purchased a building at 3449 South Grand Boulevard in St. Louis. The property in Houston was to be sold.

In connection with the new headquarters, the organization established the Pentecostal Publishing House, and, for the first time since 1935, owned its publishing facilities. As operating capital, the Executive Board voted to borrow $1,500 from the Apostolic Pentecostal Church in St. Louis.[36]

In 1945 there were seven officials and staff members at headquarters.

CHRISTIAN EDUCATION

The Pentecostal Church, Incorporated showed only sporadic interest in this phase of God's work. Its first school was known as

[35] Ibid., September, 1939, p. 3.
[36] Minutes, Executive Board, 1945.

The Pentecostal Bible Training School

When officials of the organization purchased the large hotel in Louisiana, Missouri, they had in mind the starting of a school. On January 15, 1934, the school was opened, with twelve students. The Reverend and Mrs. Merle Hendrickson came from Williams, Arizona to teach. The curriculum consisted of arithmetic, spelling, English, penmanship, public speaking, church history, theology, pastoral theology, and singing. The first term lasted six months.[37]

The school was moved to Dallas in 1934, but was closed in 1935, due to the lack of support.[38]

Northwest Bible and Training School

This school was located in Caldwell, Idaho. It was directed by E. Rohn, well known minister of the organization. The school was officially recognized in September, 1939.[39]

Intermountain Christian Institute

Founded and operated by another well-known minister, A. D. Hurt, this school, located in Boise, Idaho, was recognized by the organization in October, 1940. Subjects taught were Bible, English, music, and commercial courses.[40]

Pentecostal Bible Institute

Plans were made in the 1944 General Conference to establish this school. A. L. Clanton said, "Perhaps the most progressive move of the conference was the adopting of a policy for Institutions of Learning, and the forming of a national Bible school, to be known as the Pentecostal Bible Institute." [41]

Property consisting of several suitable buildings was purchased in Tupelo, Mississippi. C. D. Soper, who had been

---

[37] Apostolic Herald, January, 1934, p. 2.
[38] Ibid., June, 1935, p. 4.
[39] Ibid., September, 1939, p. 3.
[40] Ibid., November, 1940, p. 5.
[41] Ibid., December, 1944, p. 14.

active in Bible school work in Idaho, was appointed Principal. The school opened for its first term on October 12, 1945.

History of the school will be continued in chapter eleven.

Board of Christian Education

This board, to consist of from three to seven members, was created at the 1940 General Conference.

Its duties were to make a thorough study of the nature and problems of the education of Pentecostal youth, and to direct the policies of the organization's educational program, as prescribed by the Executive Board. A. D. Gurley, S. C. McClain and Dan Hayes were appointed as the first members.[42]

This was a step in the right direction. The organization was awakening to the need of Christian education.

GROWTH

The Pentecostal Church, Incorporated enjoyed a steady, though not phenomenal, growth throughout its history.

In 1940, W. E. Kidson wrote, "We are glad to report that during the first eight months of this year . . . we have had an increase in new members of more than twenty percent . . . Part of the credit is due to the efforts of our General Superintendent, Howard A. Goss, who has been on the field continually. . . ."[43]

The 1945 Manual of the Pentecostal Church, Incorporated shows 810 Ministers and 175 churches. The list of churches included only those which were affiliated. These, along with the non-affiliated churches, totaled approximately 500.[44]

---

[42] Ibid., November, 1940, p. 5.
[43] Ibid., September, 1940, p. 4.
[44] Oscar Vouga, Personal Interview.

9
Unsuccessful Attempts at Merger

This book has already mentioned three mergers among Oneness Pentecostals. First, there was the merger of the General Assembly of the Apostolic Assemblies and the Pentecostal Assemblies of the World; second, the consolidation of Emmanuel's Church in Jesus Christ and the Apostolic Churches (or Church) of Jesus Christ; and third, the coming together of the Apostolic Church of Jesus Christ and the Pentecostal Assemblies of the World. Each of these mergers was more involved than the one preceding it, since the movements continued to grow numerically, and in complexity of organization.

The greatest merger of all was yet to come—that of the Pentecostal Assemblies of Jesus Christ and the Pentecostal Church, Incorporated. Chapter ten will relate, in detail, the account of this merger.

But there were also unsuccessful attempts at merger—unsuccessful in the sense that they fell short of realization. On the other hand, they cannot be classed as total failures, for they revealed the deep longing of God's Oneness people for unity and organic union.

The First Attempt

On page three of the Pentecostal Witness for December, 1926, was this bold headline: CONSOLIDATION OF EMMANUEL'S CHURCH IN JESUS CHRIST AND PENTE-

COSTAL MINISTERIAL ALLIANCE AT PRESENT IMPOSSIBLE.

W. H. Lyon, Chairman of Emmanuel's Church in Jesus Christ, had met with officials of the Pentecostal Ministerial Alliance in Benton, Arkansas at their state convention a short time before.

Lyon wrote: ". . . There was no progress made toward a unifying and consolidation of the two movements, as the officials of the Pentecostal Ministerial Alliance desired that we submerge into their body. This we were not at all inclined to do, since most of the Southern brethren were not pleased to have it so, and are now satisfied with Emmanuel's Church in Jesus Christ." [1]

Officials of the Pentecostal Ministerial Alliance felt that, since their organization had been formed first, ministers of Emmanuel's Church in Jesus Christ should join it, thus achieving unity. This feeling was revealed in a letter sent out in December, 1926, from St. Paul, Minnesota, by certain officials of the Pentecostal Ministerial Alliance, to ministers of Emmanuel's Church in Jesus Christ. But to these ministers, this was not a valid reason for dissolving their organization, by joining, either collectively or individually, the Pentecostal Ministerial Alliance.[2]

Consolidation Conference Announced

In May, 1927, Chairman Lyon of Emmanuel's Church in Jesus Christ announced a conference in Norphlet, Arkansas, May 10-16, for the purpose of meeting with officials of the Apostolic Churches of Jesus Christ, with headquarters in St. Louis, in hopes that an agreement could be reached to consolidate the two bodies.[3]

There is no record that this meeting took place. Perhaps

[1] Pentecostal Witness, December, 1926, p. 3.
[2] Ibid., January, 1927, p. 1.
[3] Ibid., May, 1927, p. 9.

it was postponed, for it was in October of that same year that the two groups did meet, and voted to consolidate.

An Invitation Extended

While in their fourth annual General Assembly at Little Rock, Arkansas, in October, 1928, the Pentecostal Ministerial Alliance received an invitation from Chairman Lyon of Emmanuel's Church in Jesus Christ to send a representative to Pt. Arthur, Texas to discuss consolidation of the two bodies. Howard Goss was delegated to accept the invitation.

After attending, Goss said, ". . . the Emmanuel's Church brethren did not, as a whole, agree to the consolidation, so the matter was dropped." [4]

This was the same meeting in which Emmanuel's Church in Jesus Christ consummated its merger with the Apostolic Churches of Jesus Christ (chapter 5, page 60). It was apparently their intention at this time to include the Pentecostal Ministerial Alliance in the merger, but such did not materialize.

An Exchange of Letters

The next unsuccessful move toward merger was made by the ministers of the Apostolic Church of Jesus Christ in their fifth annual General Conference, held in Louann, Arkansas, September 29 – October 5, 1930. They sought to merge with the Pentecostal Ministerial Alliance.

The group passed the following: "In pursuance with the unanimous sentiment of this convention favoring a greater unity among all Oneness folk and movements, be it resolved, That A. H. Beisner, James A. Frush, Ben Pemberton, L. R. Ooton, and W. H. Whittington represent the Apostolic Church of Jesus Christ in working with others to this end." [5]

This resolution soon led to the writing of the following letter: [6]

[4] Ibid., November, 1928, p. 5.
[5] Ibid., December, 1930, p. 6.
[6] Ibid., September – October, 1930, p. 1.

APOSTOLIC CHURCH OF JESUS CHRIST, INC.
St. Louis, Missouri

October 20th, 1930.

The Pentecostal Ministerial Alliance,
In Convention Assembled,
3109 Cass Avenue,
St. Louis, Missouri.

Dear Brethren:

Sincere Christian greetings to you in the precious name of the Lord Jesus Christ!

Recognizing the worth and importance of a greater unity among all "Oneness" people and movements, believing that Pentecost can only be repeated when church leaders are truly in the unity of the spirit, and that the time has come when we need to cut ourselves loose from the dogmas of organizations that have retarded the development of His church, that in these strenuous times of the last days extra effort is essential to draw attention to this condition, and further believing that an earnest effort should be made at this time under the direction of competent leadership in this connection, to do this:

We, the undersigned members of a Committee, authorized and representing The Apostolic Church of Jesus Christ, Inc., consistent with the unanimous action of the annual convention held in Louann, Arkansas, September 29th to October 5th, 1930, here and now, pledge our hearty support to the enterprise and earnestly covet and respectfully solicit the co-operation of The Pentecostal Ministerial Alliance, to this end, and:

We agree, to serve in such other capacity in conjunction with The Pentecostal Ministerial Alliance and others, as may be mutually desirable in advancing the objective of the movement for the amalgamation of all "Jesus Only" people and movements compatible with the Bible truth.

COMMITTEE
FOR THE APOSTOLIC CHURCH OF JESUS CHRIST, INC.
ST. LOUIS, MISSOURI

James A. Frush	*Ben Pemberton*
W. H. Whittington	*L. R. Ooton*
	A. H. Beisner

To this letter, the Presbyter Board of the Pentecostal Ministerial Alliance, which was assembled in General Conference, sent the following reply: [7]

THE PENTECOSTAL MINISTERIAL ALLIANCE
Incorporated

October 21, 1930

The Apostolic Church of Jesus Christ,
St. Louis, Missouri
Attention A. H. Beisner, Chairman

Dear Sir:
 Greetings in the Name of our Risen Lord!
 We, the Presbyter Board of the Pentecostal Ministerial Alliance, Inc., of Louisiana, Mo., received your letter of October 20th, which expresses your desire for unity.

 We, too, are hungry for the time when all clean, spirit-filled ministers might be united in one great organization for the upbuilding of the kingdom of our Lord. We believe we have at this time the foundation of the best working order to bring about the upbuilding of the kingdom of any organization in existence at the present time, and since it is possible to make whatever changes may be deemed necessary in our by-laws, we do not know of any better proposition to make than to offer fellowship to all worthy ministers who might meet the requirements of our organization. After being admitted to fellowship, each one naturally would have an opportunity to help to change or mold the future of our organization.

 Naturally, since we are all human, there are weak points. These we are attempting to remedy from time to time. Our brethren are well pleased with the progress we have made and we feel that we have the presence of the Lord in our midst. We appreciate the sincerity of any of your true members, and pray that the time will soon come when all may be united into one great army battling against the powers of darkness.

Yours in the Master's Service,
Chairman, Dan Hayes,
Secretary, A. D. Gurley.

WEK:DB

[7] Ibid., p. 2.

On the day following, the committee from the Apostolic Church of Jesus Christ sent its second letter to the officials of the Pentecostal Ministerial Alliance. It read: [8]

THE APOSTOLIC CHURCH OF JESUS CHRIST
St. Louis, Missouri

October 22nd, 1930

The Pentecostal Ministerial Alliance,
In Convention Assembled.
3109 Cass Avenue.
St. Louis, Missouri.

Dear Brethren: —

Greetings to you in the worthy name of the Lord Jesus!

We beg to acknowledge receipt of a communication handed to me by your secretary, under date of October 21st, 1930, dictated by "WEK" and signed by the chairman and secretary of the P.M.A. board of presbyters, in which, reply is made to the request for unity and co-operation; looking forward to the amalgamation of all "oneness" folk and movements, by a committee representing The Apostolic Church of Jesus Christ, Inc., St. Louis, Missouri.

In reply the Committee would have you know that it is keenly disappointed by your action, wherein, you fail to join in this most needed and altruistic endeavor.

Furthermore, we beg to state; undismayed, we are pledged to a maximum effort to the final culmination of the objective stated in our first communication. All with the hope of bringing about this paramount need in these last days.

Yours very sincerely,
A. H. Beisner.

---

[8] Ibid.

In their letter, the officials of the Pentecostal Ministerial Alliance had expressed themselves as being ". . . hungry for the time when all clean, Spirit-filled ministers might be united in one great organization. . . ." But once again they had advanced the idea that the best way to bring this about was for other ministers to join their organization.

In its second letter, the committee from the Apostolic Church of Jesus Christ expressed keen disappointment at the unsuccessful merger attempt.

The Unity Conference

The next attempt at merger came in September, 1931. A Unity Conference was announced for September 29 – October 4, to be held at 50 Hayden Avenue, in Columbus, Ohio.[9]

The notice read, "Many of the leading ministers of the great Pentecostal movement have long felt the need of a real get-together Bible conference . . . The mighty Pentecostal power is lacking in our midst. Division among brethren is one of the primary causes of this.

"The names below are just a few of the brethren favorable to this conference: A. H. Beisner; H. A. Goss; Frank Small; M. R. Tatman; W. T. Witherspoon; Stanley Hanby; F. E. Curts; W. K. Hoag; T. C. Davis; J. C. Brickey; O. F. Fauss; and J. A. Frush." [10]

Four Oneness organizations were represented at the Columbus meeting: The Pentecostal Assemblies of the World; the Pentecostal Ministerial Alliance; The Apostolic Church of Jesus Christ; and the Apostolic Church of Pentecost of Canada.[11]

In the meeting, a resolution was passed unanimously to bend every effort toward an amalgamation of all Jesus' name organizations.[12]

[9] Ibid., September, 1931, p. 13.
[10] Ibid.
[11] Ibid., October – November, 1931, p. 4.
[12] Ibid.

Another Unsuccessful Attempt

Following the Columbus Unity Conference, the ministers of the Apostolic Church of Jesus Christ went to St. Louis for their sixth annual General Conference, to be held October 6-11, 1931.

As they were anticipating an amalgamation with the Pentecostal Ministerial Alliance, no new business was done. They even postponed the election of officers, feeling sure that a merger would be consummated. The October issue of the Pentecostal Witness was delayed, in order to carry the news, and a combined October-November issue was printed.[13]

On October 19, the members of the committee appointed by the Apostolic Church of Jesus Christ again made their way to St. Louis, to attend the Pentecostal Ministerial Alliance General Conference.[14]

In this conference, the Pentecostal Ministerial Alliance passed the following: "Resolved, That our official board be authorized to act as a committee to consider, and consummate, if possible, an amalgamation with the Apostolic Church of Jesus Christ, the terms to be ratified by our present General Conference. The following Bible truths are to be the basis of fellowship: Jesus, the Mighty God; water baptism in His name; and the baptism of the Holy Ghost, with the evidence of speaking with other tongues." [15]

The General Board met as a committee, and on October 21, brought to the assembled conference the following conditions for merger:

"Resolved, That we recommend the name of the amalgamated body shall be the Pentecostal Ministerial Alliance of the Apostolic Church of Jesus Christ.

"Resolved, That we recommend that the Pentecostal Witness and the Apostolic Herald merge under the name of the Apostolic Herald.

[13] Ibid.
[14] Ibid.
[15] Apostolic Herald, November, 1931, p. 5.

"Resolved, That we recommend that the present discipline and bylaws of the Pentecostal Ministerial Alliance remain in force for the consolidated body." [16]

The General Conference of the Pentecostal Ministerial Alliance then voted in favor of a merger, upon the basis of the foregoing stipulations.

On October 22, in a joint meeting with the ministers of the Apostolic Church of Jesus Christ, the recommendations were read, but were not brought before the joint session for a vote.[17] As the recommendations had already been accepted by the ministers of the Pentecostal Ministerial Alliance, the failure to bring the matter to a vote must have been caused by the reluctance of the Apostolic Church of Jesus Christ ministers.

It is not hard to see their reasons for this, when one considers the merger requirements. Frush wrote: "We were willing to make many concessions, but certain things were demanded that we could not see our way clear to accept. . . ." [18]

The Final Failure

It appears that no further official move toward merger was made until 1936. By then, the group formerly known as the Apostolic Church of Jesus Christ had become the Pentecostal Assemblies of Jesus Christ (see page 69). And the Pentecostal Ministerial Alliance had changed its name to Pentecostal Church, Incorporated (page 87).

On this occasion, ministers of the Pentecostal Church, Incorporated had approached ministers of the Pentecostal Assemblies of Jesus Christ, desiring dialogue on the possibility of unity. In its fifth General Conference, held in Columbus, Ohio, September 14-20, 1936, this latter organization passed the following:

"Be it resolved, That out of consideration for the members of the Pentecostal Church, Incorporated, who have evidenced

---

[16] Ibid., p. 6.

[17] Ibid.

[18] Pentecostal Witness, October – November, 1931, p. 11.

their desire for unity with the Pentecostal Assemblies of Jesus Christ, we send a committee to meet with them in their convention in St. Louis, to negotiate terms and requirements for effecting the amalgamation of the two bodies." [19]

Later in the same convention it was voted to appoint the Board of Presbyters as the committee, and that the committee was to insist upon the following points:

1. The name of Jesus Christ is to be included in the name of the merged body, and that name cannot be one which can be owned by charter by any body now in existence.

2. That baptism in water in Jesus' name, and the baptism of the Holy Ghost, with the initial evidence of speaking in other tongues, be recognized as constituting the new birth, and be accepted as one of our fundamental doctrines.

3. That the merged body be governed by a Board of Presbyters.

4. That the Pentecostal Assemblies of the World, the Apostolic Church of Jesus Christ, and any other Oneness organization, be allowed to send a committee empowered to act on joining the proposed merger.

5. That the Presbyter Board of the Pentecostal Assemblies of Jesus Christ, along with the boards of all other organizations that might merge, be accepted as the governing board of the merged body, until its first General Convention.[20]

Carrying out the resolution, eight General Presbyters and the General Secretary of the Pentecostal Assemblies of Jesus Christ met in St. Louis with eight or ten General Presbyters of the Pentecostal Church, Incorporated.

According to W. T. Witherspoon, the five points were presented, and were rejected by the Pentecostal Church, Incorporated, which then offered the following counter proposals:

1. That the name of the organization be Pentecostal Churches, Incorporated, with the suggestion that the term "Incorporated" be kept in the background.

---

[19] Pentecostal Outlook, October, 1936, p. 18.
[20] Ibid., p. 19.

2. That the matter of the new birth be left open to personal conviction.

3. That there be a double organization.[21] By this, they meant that there would be a separate organization for Negroes. At this time, the Pentecostal Assemblies of Jesus Christ still had some Negro ministers, though many had gone back to the old Pentecostal Assemblies of the World.

Witherspoon said, "Their proposition (concerning the Negro ministers) had its merits, and seemed . . . to be advocated by a sincere desire for unity that would be workable in all parts of the country. This adjustment of the race question was looked upon with favor by practically all of the Pentecostal Assemblies of Jesus Christ presbyters present in the meeting." [22]

But in their General Conference shortly before, the Pentecostal Assemblies of Jesus Christ had asked certain concessions of its Negro ministers, to which these ministers had graciously consented.[23] Now, the officials did not feel that they should force these Negro ministers into a separate organization, unless they were willing. When approached, the Negro ministers declared such an arrangement unacceptable.[24]

Because of this, and because other counter proposals were also unacceptable, another attempted merger was unsuccessful.

No further official attempt would be made until 1944.

---

[21] Pentecostal Outlook, December, 1936, p. 24.
[22] Ibid.
[23] Ibid.
[24] Ibid., January, 1937, p. 21.

10
The Merger

Perhaps those unfamiliar with Oneness history will wonder why, since other mergers of different Oneness groups have already been mentioned in this book, this chapter is designated simply as THE MERGER. Should it not have been given a more specific name, distinguishing it, thereby, from other mergers?

No, for to Oneness people of this generation there is one merger that stands out above all others—that of the Pentecostal Assemblies of Jesus Christ and the Pentecostal Church, Incorporated. In fact, we could call this consolidation THE merger.

A DEEP DESIRE FOR UNITY

The coming together of these two groups was the culmination of all the heartfelt longings of hundreds of Oneness ministers and laymen—longings that had existed through the years. These desires were expressed in different ways.

Ministers Wrote of Unity

W. T. Witherspoon wrote these words: "While in prayer a few days ago, the Lord burdened me with the terrible conditions, not only in the world, but in the Jesus Only church. It seems to me that God is letting enough happen to show the brethren of like precious faith the absolute necessity of getting together, regardless of machinery or offices. No one group can point their fingers at the other. Division is keeping back God's power. The only division there should be is between righteousness and unrighteousness; holiness and sin." [1]

Later, L. R. Ooton said this: ". . . There is no greater need among the Spirit-filled children of God today, than the unity of the Spirit. There are entirely too many divisions or organizations separating Oneness brethren, and the eternal God is viewing this situation today. If we preach Oneness, it is also necessary for us to practice the same." [2]

Inter-Organizational Fellowship Increased

Ministers of one organization conducted revivals for ministers of the other. Both ministers and laymen of one group attended church services, conventions and camp meetings of the other.

To illustrate: In Louisiana, in the summer of 1934, the Pentecostal Assemblies of Jesus Christ and the Pentecostal Church, Incorporated announced a joint camp meeting, to be held in Oakdale.[3]

In that same year, Pentecostal Assemblies of Jesus Christ ministers of the Indiana District passed a resolution ". . . that we practice the unity of the Spirit by fellowshipping brethren of like precious faith, so long as their lives are consistent with the doctrine of holiness, regardless of their affiliation with other reputable organizations. . . ." [4]

Apparently this bore fruit, for we read of a later Indiana convention: "A good number of Pentecostal Church, Incorporated brethren from Illinois were with us through these meetings." And these words were added: "We hope the same spirit of fellowship will grip the hearts of others, and God's people everywhere will come together in unity." [5]

---

[1] Pentecostal Outlook, November, 1933, p. 24.
[2] Ibid., June, 1936, p. 8.
[3] Ibid., May, 1934, p. 24.
[4] Ibid., June, 1934, p. 21.
[5] G. C. Bryan, Pentecostal Outlook, July, 1936, p. 24.

By the early 1940's these desires for unity had intensified. In 1943 and 1944 there was apparently considerable dialogue among ministers of both groups relative to merger.

THE 1944 GENERAL CONFERENCES

Pentecostal Assemblies of Jesus Christ

This group had canceled its 1943 General Conference. The United States was in war, and the Director of the Office of Defense Transportation had requested all groups to cancel their 1943 meetings if possible.[6] Only General Presbyters and District Elders met.

The thirteenth annual General Conference was held September 26 – October 1, 1944, in St. Louis, at White Way Tabernacle, where Walter S. Guinn was pastor.

Harry Branding, well known leader in the Pentecostal Church, Incorporated, and pastor of Apostolic Pentecostal Church in St. Louis, visited this conference. Hearing a renowned Bible teacher give a Bible lesson, he saw that the two groups were basically identical in doctrine.

"Knowing that Oliver F. Fauss, minister in the Pentecostal Assemblies of Jesus Christ, had quite a lot of influence, he approached him with the idea of a merger. His words were, 'Why not get together?' He told Fauss that if the Pentecostal Assemblies of Jesus Christ would pass some kind of legislation toward it, he would use all the power he had to accomplish the same end in the next conference of the Pentecostal Church, Incorporated."[7]

Initial action was taken at once. The Pentecostal Assemblies of Jesus Christ passed the following:

"Inasmuch as several of our officials have been approached during the past year by several of the officials of the Pentecostal Church, Incorporated in regard to the possibility of merger of the two organizations,

[6] Pentecostal Outlook, August, 1943, p. 1.
[7] Foster, "Think It Not Strange," p. 84.

"Be it Resolved, That we extend the Pentecostal Church, Incorporated an invitation on the part of their officials to suggest a meeting with the officials of the Pentecostal Assemblies of Jesus Christ, to discuss necessary steps to bring about such a merger.

"Be it further Resolved, That the Presbyter Board and General Secretary-Treasurer be authorized to negotiate and merge with the Pentecostal Church, Incorporated." [8]

Pentecostal Church, Incorporated

A short time later, October 24-31, 1944, the Pentecostal Church, Incorporated assembled at Jonesboro, Arkansas, in Bible Hour Tabernacle, where T. Richard Reed was pastor, for its twentieth annual General Conference.

In response to the invitation from the Pentecostal Assemblies of Jesus Christ, the conference ". . . expressed its desire for the unity of all . . . Jesus' name groups, but specified only the Pentecostal Assemblies of Jesus Christ, thereby authorizing its General Board to negotiate the merger. . . ." [9]

Thus the first hurdle toward consolidation was cleared.

A JOINT COMMITTEE APPOINTED

At its General Conference in 1944, each organization appointed a committee of three to meet jointly, and take the necessary preliminary steps toward effecting the merger. From the Pentecostal Assemblies of Jesus Christ there were W. T. Witherspoon, S. R. Hanby, and O. F. Fauss. Committee members from the Pentecostal Church, Incorporated were H. A. Goss, Oscar Vouga, and B. H. Hite. [10]

The First Committee Meeting

The committee met first on January 30, 1945, upstairs in the headquarters building of the Pentecostal Church,

[8] Hanby, Pentecostal Outlook, November, 1944, p. 17.
[9] Goss, Apostolic Herald, September, 1945, p. 7.
[10] Pentecostal Outlook, June, 1945, p. 4.

Incorporated, at 3449 South Grand Boulevard, St. Louis, Missouri.[11]

These men had been ministers in their respective organizations for many years. They knew, therefore, that the main problem to be worked out concerned the fundamental doctrine of the proposed new organization.

It was brought out in chapters seven and eight that both the Pentecostal Church, Incorporated and the Pentecostal Assemblies of Jesus Christ believed in repentance, water baptism in the name of Jesus Christ, and the receiving of the Holy Ghost, with the initial sign of speaking with other tongues. To be a minister in either organization, one must have obeyed these gospel precepts, and must teach and preach them.

But in general, the two groups differed in the spiritual significance attached to each of these "steps" in the plan of salvation. The vast majority of the ministers in the Pentecostal Assemblies of Jesus Christ believed that water baptism in Jesus' name remitted sins, and was the birth of the water. They further believed that the baptism of the Holy Ghost was the birth of the Spirit.

The belief of some in the Pentecostal Church, Incorporated was identical with this. Others, however, believed that the word "for" in Acts 2:38 meant "because of," and that one was baptized because his sins had been remitted, through the efficacy of Jesus' shed blood, at the time of repentance. The Pentecostal Church, Incorporated had accepted ministers who believed either way, seeking to keep the unity of the Spirit, until they all came into the unity of the faith.

So it is easy to see that before a merger could be effected, there must be a fundamental doctrine, relative to the plan of salvation, that ministers in both groups could conscientiously accept.

After some discussion, Witherspoon left the committee

---

[11] Minutes of the Committee.

room, went downstairs to the Pentecostal Publishing House, borrowed a typewriter, and wrote the following Fundamental Doctrine: [12]

> The basic and fundamental doctrine of this organization shall be the Bible standard of full salvation, which is repentance, baptism in water by immersion in the name of the Lord Jesus Christ, and the baptism of the Holy Ghost with the initial sign of speaking with other tongues as the Spirit gives utterance.
>
> We shall endeavor to keep the unity of the Spirit until we all come into the unity of the faith, at the same time admonishing all brethren that they shall not contend for their different views to the disunity of the body.[13]

Surely he was inspired of God that day. The members of the committee accepted this statement of fundamental doctrine. Later, it was passed by both General Boards, and was finally adopted by both General Conferences. Through the years it has stood as originally adopted.

It was agreed by the members of the joint committee that considerable time could be saved by their meeting again at a later date to revise the two disciplines (manuals), and have the revised edition ready for the perusal of the joint meetings of the two General Boards, to be held later.[14]

The Second Committee Meeting

The Committee on Revision met March 20, 1945, again at 3449 South Grand Boulevard. At this meeting, the members were Howard A. Goss, A. O. Moore, Oscar Vouga (of the Pentecostal Church, Incorporated); Oliver F. Fauss, and Irvin I. Bradley (of the Pentecostal Assemblies of Jesus Christ).

The committee revised and consolidated the two manuals,

---

[12] Interview with Oscar Vouga, Committee Secretary.
[13] Manual, United Pentecostal Church, 1969, p. 24.
[14] Pentecostal Outlook, June, 1945, p. 4.

and made the new constitution and bylaws ready for the joint session of the two boards.

JOINT GENERAL BOARD MEETINGS

The General Boards of the two organizations met jointly in Apostolic Pentecostal Church at St. Louis, Missouri, April 17-20, 1945. Of these meetings, W. T. Witherspoon wrote to the ministers in his group:

"Prior to the coming together of all the delegates of both organizations, your Board of Presbyters had three or four meetings with the General Board of the Pentecostal Church, Incorporated. There were a number of major points which they wished to discuss. At times we diametrically disagreed, as we presented our views, based upon what we thought you would want. A sweet spirit of unity and forbearance swept away each disagreement, as we met each other half way." [15]

Headquarters for the New Organization

There was no controversy over the location of the headquarters of the merged body. The Pentecostal Church, Incorporated had what was, at that time, an adequate building, advantageously located, and well arranged. And, as you will perhaps recall from chapter seven, the Pentecostal Assemblies of Jesus Christ had no headquarters building housing its various departments.

The New Name

"Next came the matter of the name of the new organization. This point was perhaps the most strongly argued. It was the contention of many that the word *Pentecostal* should not be used because of the reproach borne by that name in many places. Against this it was argued that the word *Apostolic* was also much discredited in many places. Further, it was the name of certain groups that were not Oneness. Then, too, it

---

[15] Ibid., October, 1945, p. 5.

would be hard to choose a name containing the word *Apostolic* that had not already been copyrighted.

"At this point in the argument, it was suggested that there was a vast difference between the significance of the word *Pentecost* and *Pentecostal.* The first refers only to the initial experience received upon that particular day, while the second includes the initial experience and all that pertains to it, that is, a godly life, the teaching of the Epistles, etc. This makes the word *Pentecostal* practically synonymous with *Apostolic.*"

It was at this point in the meeting that the name *United Pentecostal Church* was agreed upon.[16]

Howard Goss said of these meetings: ". . . when the General Boards met together for several days, we were able to reach an understanding and an agreement on principles and doctrines. . . ." [17]

The two boards adjourned their joint meeting, with the understanding that the matter of merger would be taken up at the next General Conferences.

THE 1945 GENERAL CONFERENCES

Never in the history of the groups had they met in the same city at the same time. But both organizations scheduled their 1945 General Conferences for St. Louis, September 20 to 26. This meeting plan had been agreed upon by the two General Boards, to facilitate the expected merger.

The Pentecostal Church, Incorporated

This organization met in Kiel Auditorium.

During one business meeting, it was moved that, in the event the merger was consummated, the former two bodies would choose, by a majority vote, between the two names: United Pentecostal Church, and Apostolic Pentecostal Church.

[16] Witherspoon, Pentecostal Outlook, October, 1945, p. 5.
[17] Minutes, P. C. I. General Conference, 1945.

123

This motion was defeated.[18] The group then voted unanimously to accept the name suggested by the two General Boards: United Pentecostal Church.[19]

A motion was made to take the word "full" out of the Fundamental Doctrine, but was defeated.[20]

The Pentecostal Church, Incorporated also voted to accept the proposed name, the Pentecostal Herald, for the official organ of the new organization.[21]

Of this conference, Ethel Goss wrote: "The smile of God seemed to be upon this union (the merger), as whatever questions or adjustments arose, they were quickly, easily and sweetly settled to the pleasure of all. Some who, before the conference, for various reasons, could not see how it would work out satisfactorily, when they saw how easily God slipped us past all the shoals and hidden snags, felt a mounting confidence in God . . . and decided to help see it through." [22]

The Pentecostal Church, Incorporated had already passed a resolution that the vote on the merger must be by a two-thirds majority to carry. When the question was finally brought to a vote on Monday, September 24, the vote was 164 for, and 24 against. It was moved to make the yes vote unanimous, and the motion carried.[23]

The Pentecostal Assemblies of Jesus Christ

The ministers of this organization met for their day sessions in White Way Tabernacle, where Walter S. Guinn was pastor. Each night, and for the Sunday afternoon foreign missionary service, they assembled in a joint meeting with the Pentecostal Church, Incorporated in Kiel Auditorium.

Of these joint evening services, W. T. Witherspoon wrote: "The coming together of the two bodies seemed to add new life

[18] Ibid.
[19] Ibid.
[20] Ibid.
[21] Ibid.
[22] Apostolic Herald, November, 1945, p. 9.
[23] Minutes, P. C. I. General Conference, 1945.

and enthusiasm to our activities. I wish you could have all been there and attended those wonderful evangelistic services. Each night a Pentecostal Church, Incorporated and a Pentecostal Assemblies of Jesus Christ minister preached. The spirit of division just seemed to melt away in the presence of God's united people worshipping together as one. I have attended many conventions, but I do not recall one where the Spirit of God worked so mightily as this last convention, when God's ministers resolved to stand together in a common cause." [24]

During the day sessions of the Pentecostal Assemblies of Jesus Christ, the proposed constitution and bylaws, passed the preceding April by the combined General Boards, were read, and explanations given. Stanley R. Hanby, General Secretary, was also asked to read certain resolutions which the two boards had passed, pertaining to the merger.

The group then voted to adopt the proposed constitution and resolutions, with the exception of the suggested name — United Pentecostal Church. Three names were presented for consideration: United Pentecostal Church, United Apostolic Church, and United Church of Christ. A majority of the group voted for the name United Apostolic Church. But these words were added: "However, be it understood that this recommendation in no way means a block to the merger of the two organizations." [25] One must appreciate such humility. They were willing to give up the name they desired, in order to merge.

In the 2:00 p. m. business meeting on Monday, September 24, General Chairman Witherspoon ". . . announced that he had just received word that the Pentecostal Church, Incorporated had voted, by a big majority, to merge with the Pentecostal Assemblies of Jesus Christ. The announcement was received with joy." [26]

---

[24] Pentecostal Outlook, October, 1945, p. 5.
[25] Ibid., p. 3.
[26] Ibid., p. 4.

The Pentecostal Assemblies of Jesus Christ then adjourned its business session, planning to meet jointly with the Pentecostal Church, Incorporated on the following day, to consummate the merger.

THE JOINT CONFERENCE SESSION

On Tuesday morning, September 25, the two organizations came together in their first joint business meeting, to officially merge, and elect officers for the united body.

During this meeting, "It was moved that the conference go on record as accepting the name United Pentecostal Church. This carried unanimously." [27] Thus the combined body, once and for all, adopted the name that it was to wear throughout its history.

The New Officials

Howard A. Goss was practically the unanimous choice for General Superintendent. W. T. Witherspoon declined to give up his pastorate and leave Columbus, Ohio, but he was chosen Assistant General Superintendent. Stanley W. Chambers was elected General Secretary-Treasurer. He had been in the former Pentecostal Assemblies of Jesus Christ not quite five years, but it was voted to waive the five-year requirement for that conference only, that he might be elected, since he was deemed extremely well qualified for the office. Other officials elected were: T. R. Dungan, Assistant General Secretary and Publishing House Manager; Wynn T. Stairs, Foreign Missionary Secretary; M. J. Wolff, Editor; and Paul H. Box, Assistant Editor.

Thus began the greatest of all Oneness Pentecostal organizations—The United Pentecostal Church.

Witherspoon well summed up the successful merger with these words: "Truly it was nothing less than supernatural, the way the blessed Spirit of God enabled the brethren to over-

---

[27] Minutes of Merged Body, September 25, 1945.

come. It means more than the average preacher can understand to bring about the uniting of two such bodies, with the many, many matters that have to be considered. There were practically no dissenting voices, and as we look back over the proceedings of the convention, we can only exclaim, 'What hath God wrought!'" [28]

---

[28] Pentecostal Outlook, October, 1945, p. 5.

11
The United Pentecostal Church

The merger of the Pentecostal Assemblies of Jesus Christ and the Pentecostal Church, Incorporated brought about the largest Oneness Pentecostal organization ever. Initially, there were 1,838 ministers and approximately 900 churches.

Of the merger, M. J. Wolff, first editor, said, "It was said of prohibition, 'It was a noble experiment.' Some have said the same thing about the merger, and then added, 'That's all it will be.' But God has certainly blessed this step of faith and obedience." [1]

General Superintendent Howard A. Goss declared, "This unifying of the two bodies has been one of the greatest steps ever taken by the Pentecostal people. Our prayer is that we shall continue to work for the unity of all good clean brethren, but we are especially interested in working for a greater peace and harmony among ourselves. . . ." [2]

Assistant General Superintendent W. T. Witherspoon spoke in the same vein: "I for one am happy indeed over the merger. I fully recognize the many difficulties and perplexing problems that will have to be met before things are running smoothly, but one thing I know: unity is of God. God grant that every one of us may contribute to the unity of the brethren by following peace with all men, and holiness, without which no man shall see the Lord." [3]

---

[1] The Pentecostal Herald, August, 1946, p. 2.
[2] Ibid., December, 1945, p. 11.
[3] Ibid., January, 1946, p. 2.

A small group of ministers, opposed to the merger, attempted to continue the Pentecostal Assemblies of Jesus Christ. Of this group, Witherspoon said, "When the merger was consummated, it was agreed that the charter of the Pentecostal Assemblies of Jesus Christ should become the property of the United Pentecostal Church. Unfortunately, the matter of small yearly dues was overlooked, making it possible for anyone to take up the charter by paying the past dues. This has been done, and the impression given that those who now hold the charter represent the former Pentecostal Assemblies of Jesus Christ." [4]

THE GENERAL ORGANIZATION

When two large church bodies merge, there is always much work to be done before the new organization can function smoothly and efficiently. This was certainly true in the case of the United Pentecostal Church. Much prayer and effort have gone into the making of the organization what it is today.

In the beginning, the United Pentecostal Church was governed by articles of faith and bylaws which had come from the harmonizing of the manuals of the two former organizations. Later, certain changes were made in these bylaws, and others were added, as the need arose.

The General Conference

This is the organization's annual general meeting, held in some major city in the United States. In both the 1959 and 1969 General Conferences, resolutions were introduced to make the meeting biennial, instead of annual. These resolutions were overwhelmingly defeated, showing the high esteem in which General Conferences are held.

The General Conference is the foremost authority of the organization. At this meeting reports are given, general offi-

[4] Ibid., February, 1947, p. 2.

cials are elected or appointed, motions and resolutions are discussed and acted upon, policies are adopted for the betterment of the work, and actions of the various boards and committees are presented for ratification.

The General Conference is not devoted entirely to business. Much of the time is spent in spiritual worship. It is this aspect of the meeting that causes thousands to look forward to it each year.

Places and dates of General Conferences are given below.

1945 – St. Louis, Missouri (Merger Conference)
1946 – St. Louis, Missouri – September 15 – 22
1947 – Dallas, Texas – October 22 – 30
1948 – Long Beach, California – September 8 – 16
1949 – Duluth, Minnesota – September 22 – 28
1950 – Little Rock, Arkansas – October 6 – 11
1951 – St. Louis, Missouri – September 21 – 26
1952 – Little Rock, Arkansas – October 23 – 29
1953 – St. Louis, Missouri – September 17 – 23
1954 – Columbus, Ohio – September 17 – 22
1955 – Tulsa, Oklahoma – September 23 – 28
1956 – Memphis, Tennessee – October 19 – 24
1957 – Little Rock, Arkansas – October 18 – 23
1958 – Indianapolis, Indiana – October 17 – 22
1959 – St. Louis, Missouri – September 25 – 30
1960 – Dallas, Texas – September 30 – October 5
1961 – Kansas City, Missouri – October 20 – 25
1962 – Columbus, Ohio – October 5 – 10
1963 – Memphis, Tennessee – October 10 – 15
1964 – San Antonio, Texas – October 8 – 13
1965 – Grand Rapids, Michigan – October 21 – 26
1966 – New Orleans, Louisiana – October 20 – 25
1967 – Tulsa, Oklahoma – October 19 – 24
1968 – Atlantic City, New Jersey – October 24 – 29
1969 – St. Louis, Missouri – October 23 – 28
1970 – Portland, Oregon – August 6 – 11

The General Superintendent

This is the title given the official head of the United Pentecostal Church. He supervises all the organization's general work. He presides at General Conference business meetings and General and Executive Board meetings, appoints committees, and signs every credential, license, fellowship card, and church certificate. His duties are many, and varied.

Pentecostal pioneer Howard A. Goss was elected first General Superintendent in 1945. In 1951 he was replaced by Arthur T. Morgan, who served until October 18, 1967, when he died suddenly while presiding over a General Board meeting in Tulsa, Oklahoma. The General Board appointed Oliver F. Fauss to serve as General Superintendent until January 1, 1968. At that time Stanley W. Chambers, who had been elected General Superintendent in the 1967 General Conference, took office.

The Assistant General Superintendents

At the General Conference in 1945, only one Assistant General Superintendent was elected. But in the 1951 General Conference it was voted to have two, one to reside in the Eastern Zone (the area east of the Mississippi River), the other in the Western Zone (the area west of the Mississippi).[5]

In the 1960 General Conference, the bylaw requiring each Assistant General Superintendent to live within the zone he served was repealed. This made it permissible to elect either Assistant from anywhere in the United States, with this exception: both could not reside within the same district.[6]

But in 1963, the General Conference again reversed itself, and made it mandatory that each Assistant live in the zone he served.[7]

The Assistant General Superintendents are to work under the supervision and direction of the General Superintendent,

[5] Ibid. November, 1951, p. 9.
[6] Minutes, 1960 General Conference.
[7] Ibid., 1963.

First General Board of the United Pentecostal Church

performing such duties as the work of the organization demands.[8] The General Superintendent has the authority to delegate either Assistant to serve anywhere.[9]

The first Assistant General Superintendent was W. T. Witherspoon, who was elected in 1945. When he died in 1947, he was succeeded by Oliver F. Fauss. Oscar Vouga, another well-known minister, was elected in 1949.

When it was decided to have two Assistant General Superintendents, Vouga was elected to serve in the Eastern Zone, and Fauss in the Western Zone. Ralph G. Cook became Assistant General Superintendent of the Eastern Zone in 1962, when Vouga was chosen to fill another executive office.

The General Secretary-Treasurer

The duties of this official are too well-known to detail here. As Secretary, he takes minutes, preserves records, signs documents, and can be designated by the General Superintendent to represent him in District Conferences.

As Treasurer, he receives and disburses general funds of the organization, keeping an accurate record.

Stanley W. Chambers was elected first Secretary-Treasurer of the organization in 1945, and held the office until he was elected General Superintendent in 1967. At that time he was succeeded by Cleveland M. Becton.

The Board of General Presbyters (General Board)

This board consists of the General Superintendent, the Assistant General Superintendents, the General Secretary-Treasurer, The Director of Foreign Missions, the Director of Home Missions, the Editor in Chief, the General Sunday School Director, and one General Presbyter (District Superintendent) from each organized district.

The General Board meets a few days preceding, and

---

[8] Manual, p. 36.
[9] Ibid.

during, each General Conference. Special meetings of this board can be called at any time by the General Superintendent.

Each District Superintendent is elected by his respective District Conference.

The Board of General Presbyters is the final authority on any question in the time between General Conferences. Its duties are varied, but its main function is to carry out the business of the organization according to its General Constitution, and as directed by the General Conference.

In the early days of the organization, the General Board was given the authority to amend general bylaws, or institute new ones (in harmony with the Manual), the same to become operative after having been published at least once in the Pentecostal Herald.[10]

This was later amended to give the General Board the right to only recommend such changes to the General Conference.[11]

The Executive Board

This board first consisted of the General Superintendent, the Assistant General Superintendent, the General Secretary, the Assistant General Secretary (office abolished in 1947), the Foreign Missionary Secretary, and the Editor of the Pentecostal Herald.[12]

The Manager of the Pentecostal Publishing House was added to the Executive Board in 1952.[13] In 1953 it was voted that this office not be represented on the Executive Board, since it was not essential that the one filling it be a minister.[14]

The Home Missionary Secretary (now Director of Home Missions) was added to the Executive Board in 1952.[15]

---

[10] Minutes, 1946 General Conference.
[11] Manual, 1970, p. 38.
[12] Minutes, 1946 General Conference.
[13] Ibid., 1952.
[14] Ibid., 1953.
[15] Ibid., 1952.

In 1952 a resolution was introduced to make the General Sunday School Director a member of the Executive Board, but the resolution was defeated.[16] The same was tried in 1953, and again failed.[17] But in 1969 a similar resolution was introduced, and passed without opposition.[18]

The Executive Board was then comprised of the General Superintendent, two Assistant General Superintendents, the General Secretary, the Director of Foreign Missions, the Director of Home Missions, the General Sunday School Director, and the Editor in Chief.

Perhaps one of the best definitions of the duties of this board was written in 1947: "The Executive Board functions only between meetings of the General Board. It has, at that time, authority to carry out the orders of the General Conference and the General Board, conducting the business of the organization according to the bylaws." [19]

The Executive Board usually meets twice each year. It becomes a part of the General Board when this board is in session.

Manner of Election

For the first seventeen years of the organization's history, it was required that an official receive two-thirds of the votes cast, to be elected. But in the 1962 General Conference, the following resolution was adopted: "The election of all officers in General, District and Sectional Conferences shall be by a simple majority, rather than by a two-thirds majority." [20]

All voting for officials is by secret ballot.

In any election, the first ballot is called a Nominating Ballot. If any candidate receives a two-thirds majority on this ballot, he is considered elected. If no candidate receives a two-

[16] Ibid.
[17] Ibid., 1953.
[18] Ibid., 1969.
[19] Ibid., 1947.
[20] Ibid., 1962.

thirds majority, the names of the three persons receiving the largest number of votes are presented to the conference to be voted upon. Voting continues until one of these three receives a simple majority of the votes cast.

All general officers serve for a term of two years.

Voting Constituency

Originally, the voting constituency consisted of all affiliated ministers. But in the 1956 General Conference this was passed: The voting constituency shall ". . . be all accredited ministers, with the exception of those holding local license who are not pastors or full-time evangelists."[21] This rule applied to even full-time assistant pastors holding local license.[22] The bylaw removed many local licensed ministers from the voting rolls, both in General and District Conferences.

Some felt that this rule was unconstitutional, hence a resolution was introduced in the 1957 General Conference to repeal it. The resolution was defeated.[23] A similar attempt was made in the 1966 General Conference, but it was also defeated.[24]

In addition to ministers, each affiliated local church is permitted to send one delegate to represent it at both District and General Conferences.[25]

Since 1956, missionaries on the foreign field at General Conference time have been allowed to vote for general officials by absentee ballot. Before conference time, a blank ballot is sent every missionary, upon which he writes his preference for each office. If any of his choices is nominated, his vote is applied to that candidate, so long as he is voted upon.[26]

---

[21] Ibid., 1956.
[22] Executive Board Ruling.
[23] Minutes, 1957 General Conference.
[24] Ibid., 1966.
[25] Manual, 1970, p. 94.
[26] Minutes, 1956 General Conference.

DISTRICT ORGANIZATION

Prior to the merger of the Pentecostal Assemblies of Jesus Christ and the Pentecostal Church, Incorporated, both national organizations had been divided into districts. Each of these districts was made up of one or more states. And of course, in many cases, the same geographical area was included in districts of both organizations.

General Secretary Stanley W. Chambers said, "In view of the merger, all districts will have to be reorganized under the United Pentecostal Church, and the boundaries should be agreed upon in connection with the General Superintendent and the Executive Board." [27]

Howard A. Goss, General Superintendent, immediately began this work of reorganization. During the last three months of 1945 and through the year of 1946 he organized seventeen districts.

In the beginning, some of the districts were made up of several states, due to the small number of ministers and churches in these states. Later, as the work in these districts grew, they were broken up into districts containing fewer states. Still later, these districts were reorganized, with most of them containing only single states.

In 1970 there were thirty-five districts in the United Pentecostal Church. A careful study of the following list will reveal the progressive steps of organization by which these districts were brought into their present form. The thirty-five districts mentioned above are capitalized. Dates denote when the districts were officially organized.

1945 – *North Central District* (Minnesota, Wisconsin, Iowa and Manitoba, Canada)

Northwest District (Washington, Oregon, Idaho, Wyoming, Montana, and British Columbia, Canada)

ILLINOIS DISTRICT

---

[27] Pentecostal Herald, December, 1945, p. 7.

WESTERN DISTRICT (Originally California, Arizona, and Nevada. Now only California and Nevada)

TEXICO DISTRICT (New Mexico, Colorado, and West Texas)

MISSOURI DISTRICT

TEXAS DISTRICT

1946 – LOUISIANA DISTRICT

OHIO DISTRICT

INDIANA DISTRICT (Originally included Michigan)

Southeastern District (Florida, Georgia, North Carolina)

Oklahoma-Kansas District

ARKANSAS DISTRICT

EAST CENTRAL DISTRICT (Originally Pennsylvania, Maryland, Virginia, West Virginia; now Maryland, West Virginia, and District of Columbia)

Southern District (Mississippi, Tennessee, and Alabama)

New England District (New York and New Jersey)

Maritime District (New Brunswick, Nova Scotia, Prince Edward Island, Canada)

1947 – ONTARIO DISTRICT (Originally Ontario and Quebec; now Ontario)

1949 – TENNESSEE

MISSISSIPPI

ALABAMA

MICHIGAN (Formerly part of Indiana District)

1951 – EASTERN DISTRICT (At first Connecticut, New York, New Jersey, and Eastern Pennsylvania; now New York, New Jersey and Delaware)

1954 – ARIZONA DISTRICT (Arizona was originally part of the Western District)

KENTUCKY DISTRICT

1957 — *WISCONSIN DISTRICT* (Had been part of North Central District)

1959 — *FLORIDA DISTRICT* (Formerly part of Southeastern District)

Georgia-South Carolina District (Both states had been part of Southeastern District)

1960 — *PENNSYLVANIA* (Had been part of East-Central District)

1964 — *GEORGIA* (Formerly included in Southeastern District)

Carolina District (North and South Carolina; both states formerly part of Southeastern District)

1965 — *IDAHO* (Idaho, Oregon, and Washington-British Columbia had been part of Northwest District)

OREGON

WASHINGTON-BRITISH COLUMBIA

OKLAHOMA DISTRICT

KANSAS DISTRICT (Oklahoma and Kansas districts had been together)

1966 — *PINE TREE DISTRICT* (Maine)

1967 — *MINNESOTA-MANITOBA DISTRICT*

IOWA DISTRICT

1968 — *VIRGINIA DISTRICT* (Originally part of East-Central District)

1969 — *CENTRAL NEW ENGLAND DISTRICT* (Massachusetts, Rhode Island, New Hampshire, Vermont)

NORTH CAROLINA DISTRICT

SOUTH CAROLINA DISTRICT (These two districts had formerly been one)

ROCKY MOUNTAIN DISTRICT (Montana, Wyoming, and Utah. Montana and Wyoming were originally part of the Northwest District)

District Government

Each district has an annual District Conference which serves the same purpose in the district as does the General Conference in the general organization.

In addition, each district has a District Board, consisting of the District Superintendent, the District Secretary, and the District Presbyters.

Some districts are divided into sections. In this case, the District Presbyters may be elected in Sectional Conferences.

LOCAL CHURCHES

Affiliated local churches are also recognized as part of the membership of the United Pentecostal Church. A church becomes affiliated by voting to accept the organization's Articles of Faith, and by filling in a prescribed application, which is submitted to the District Board.

MINISTERIAL MEMBERSHIP

The United Pentecostal Church has, from its inception, recognized three ministerial classifications: Local License, General License and Credential.

A Local License is issued one who is relatively new in the ministry. He must have preached an average of approximately one sermon each week for a period of six months or more. In addition, he must be at least seventeen years of age.

A General License is given one who has labored in the ministry for one full year or more, in connection with some local assembly, preaching an average of one sermon or more per week. A theological student (majoring in religion) who completes three years of Bible school training in a school endorsed by the United Pentecostal Church, and who otherwise qualifies, may be granted a General License.[28]

When one has labored actively in the ministry as a pastor or evangelist for two full consecutive years, and has been fully

---

[28] Manual, 1970, p. 41.

proven, he may be ordained, and granted a Credential. To be ordained, he must be at least twenty-one years of age.

As to doctrinal requirements, to be an affiliated minister one must have received the baptism of the Holy Ghost, have been baptized in the name of the Lord Jesus Christ, and believe in and preach the same.[29]

DOCTRINAL POSITION

It will not be possible to include in detail all the doctrines of the United Pentecostal Church. Extended comment will therefore be limited to those fundamental doctrines wherein the organization differs from all or nearly all other religious groups. Other doctrines will be given only brief mention.

The Baptism of the Holy Ghost

All members of the United Pentecostal Church believe that if one repents, and exercises faith, he will receive the baptism (gift) of the Holy Ghost. This truth is included in the organization's statement of Fundamental Doctrine, passed at the time of the merger in 1945, and found on page 121 of chapter ten.

The organization also teaches that when one receives this experience he will speak with other tongues (languages), just as the approximate one hundred and twenty did on the day of Pentecost.[30] This is a fulfillment of Isaiah 28:11 and Mark 16:17.

Baptism in Water

Another cardinal doctrine of the organization is that after one has repented, he must be baptized (immersed) in water. This baptism must be administered in Jesus' name, that is, the one baptizing must say, "I baptize you in the name of the Lord Jesus Christ." *(Note: Some ministers use shorter designations, such as "in the name of Jesus," or "Jesus Christ," or "Lord*

---

[29] Ibid., pp. 40, 41.
[30] Acts 2:4.

Jesus.") The using of this baptismal formula is one major difference between the United Pentecostal Church and all those denominations which baptize converts ". . . in the name of the Father, and of the Son, and of the Holy Ghost."

Constituents of the United Pentecostal Church believe that in Matthew 28:19 the emphasis should be placed upon the word "name"; that Jesus did not mean for anyone to repeat the titles, Father, Son and Holy Ghost as a baptismal formula; and that when one baptizes using the formula, "in the name of the Lord Jesus Christ," he is, in reality, baptizing in the *name* of the Father, and of the Son, and of the Holy Ghost.

Oneness of the Godhead

With the exception of the so-called Oneness people, nearly all of Christendom believes in what is usually designated as the Holy Trinity, affirming that there are three separate and distinct Persons in the Godhead — Father, Son, and Holy Ghost. They believe these three Persons to be coeternal and coequal, and that each is omnipotent.

Members of the United Pentecostal Church do not subscribe to the doctrine of the Trinity, declaring that neither the word Trinity, nor any teaching favoring it, is found in God's Word. In contradistinction, they affirm that there is only one Person in the Godhead. This they base upon Paul's declaration of Jesus: ". . . for in him dwelleth all the *fulness* of the Godhead *bodily"* [31]

Oneness adherents believe that God is a Spirit, [32] and, as such, is omnipresent, [33] and invisible.[34] A spirit does not have flesh and bones (a corporeal body), as is declared in Luke 24:39.

The organization rejects the doctrine that God the Father (the first Person in the Trinity) sent God the Son (the second Person) to earth to die for the sins of the world. Instead, they

---

[31] Colossians 2:9.
[32] John 4:24.
[33] Psalm 139:7-10.
[34] 1 Timothy 1:17.

affirm: "'The one true God, the Jehovah of the Old Testament, took upon Himself the form of man, and, as the son of man, was born of the Virgin Mary. As Paul says, '*God* was manifest in the flesh. . . .'"[35]

Oneness Pentecostals are not Unitarians

They, as do the Unitarians, reject the doctrine of the Trinity, but there the similarity ends. Because two groups agree on one point, certainly does not necessarily mean that they agree on others.

After rejecting the error of the Trinity, Unitarians fall prey to various other gross errors. They repudiate the Virgin birth of Jesus, they deny the divine inspiration of the Bible, they reject the atoning or sacrificial aspect of Jesus' death, and teach that salvation is by character alone. All these things are directly opposite to what Oneness Pentecostals believe. In addition, there are many other dissimilarities between Unitarians and United Pentecostals.

Other doctrines of the United Pentecostal Church can be mentioned only briefly. The group believes in the Genesis account of creation, in divine healing for the body, in the Lord's Supper (Communion), in a life of holiness, in the literal second coming of Christ, in the Millennium, in the judgment, and in an eternal heaven and hell.

The Stand Against Error

The true church of Jesus Christ has always been challenged by error. The United Pentecostal Church has had its share of these confrontations.

The Latter Rain. This erroneous doctrine first put in its appearance in 1948. Said General Superintendent Howard Goss in his annual report at General Conference: "These people claim special and new things for the Lord, teaching that the gifts of the Spirit, and laying on of hands, and the offices of the church are something new, but I know personally that the Lord

[35] Manual, 1970, p. 21.

has given the gifts of the Spirit among His people for the past fifty years." [36]

In the same meeting, Assistant General Superintendent Oscar Vouga stated: "The Latter Rain has caused a few to leave our ranks, but it has also unified the work in a better spirit and understanding." [37]

It was not until 1950, however, that the organization took an official stand against the Latter Rain movement. In February of that year the Executive Board passed a resolution condemning this error.

Following this, the 1950 General Conference passed a strong ten-point resolution, showing in detail its objections to the movement. The organization condemned (1) the promiscuous laying on of hands for the bestowing of spiritual gifts; (2) the teaching that the church is based upon present-day apostles and prophets; (3) the teaching that Christians must sever themselves from all church organization; (4) the compromising of the truths of Oneness, and water baptism in the name of Jesus Christ; (5) the teaching that one can receive the Holy Ghost without speaking with other tongues; (6) the teaching that candidates for the Holy Ghost baptism should not praise the Lord while tarrying for this gift; (7) the sowing of discord among assemblies and ministers; (8) the prophesying of prophets who speak out of their own human spirits; (9) the fellowshipping of those whose lives are ungodly; and (10) the teaching that the true church is composed of all who call themselves Christians, regardless of doctrinal belief.[38]

By taking this stand, the United Pentecostal Church soon overcame the opposition, and went on to greater victory.

The RSV Bible. The organization, in its 1953 General Conference, passed a resolution, and issued a statement, condemning the new Revised Standard Version of the Bible. Their main objection was that the new version changed certain words

[36] Minutes, 1948 General Conference.
[37] Ibid.
[38] Pentecostal Herald, November, 1950, p. 4.

First headquarters building of the United Pentecostal Church

and verses which, in effect, did away with vital fundamentals of Christian doctrine and faith, such as the Virgin birth of Christ, remission of sins, the deity of Christ, etc.[39]

The Social Gospel. In its 1965 General Conference, the United Pentecostal Church adopted a resolution which censured ". . . many major church denominations that are changing their confessions of faith, denying the fundamental truths of the Bible, and turning to science, fables and philosophies." The indictment was followed by this statement: ". . . we are opposed to the so-called social gospel. We believe in the Bible plan of salvation, which gives one a personal experience, as found in the second chapter of Acts." [40]

The Ecumenical Movement. In the same conference, the organization took a stand against the ecumenical movement, with these words: "Our hope is not in the success of the ecumenical movement, but in the second personal coming of Jesus for His church." [41]

HEADQUARTERS

In 1944 the Pentecostal Church, Incorporated had purchased for its headquarters a building at 3449 South Grand Boulevard in St. Louis. After this group merged with the Pentecostal Assemblies of Jesus Christ, this became the first headquarters of the United Pentecostal Church.

The new organization outgrew this facility almost immediately. Hence the Board of General Presbyters was authorized by the 1946 General Conference ". . . to negotiate, and to purchase new headquarters and publishing house property." [42]

On January 9, 1947, and again on January 27, the Executive Board met in St. Louis to consider a suitable location for the new headquarters.[43]

[39] Minutes, 1953 General Conference.
[40] Ibid., 1965.
[41] Ibid.
[42] Ibid., 1946.
[43] Pentecostal Herald, March, 1947, p. 6.

It was not until 1949, however, that the organization took any definite action. In April of that year, property was purchased at Gravois Avenue and Christy Park Boulevard in St. Louis.[44] The property had a 175 foot front, and was 145 feet deep. Immediately the organization began a campaign to raise funds to pay for the property and to erect a suitable headquarters building.[45]

At a meeting of the Executive Board in July, 1951, it was decided to start excavating for the basement. But in the interim, the city authorities had rezoned that part of the city, and this prohibited the building of a printing plant on the property.[46]

Fifteen months later, an unforeseen occurrence made it imperative that the organization have a new headquarters at once. On the morning of October 23, 1952, the day that the twenty-eighth General Conference began in Little Rock, the headquarters building was gutted by fire. (No vital records or publications were lost.)

The usual first orders of business were waived, so the conference could take steps to establish a new headquarters. The Building Committee recommended the purchase of property at 3645 South Grand Boulevard, just three blocks south of the old headquarters. The conference voted to buy this property, and also to sell the tract of land on Gravois.[47]

On March 1, 1954, the officials and office staff moved into the remodeled building. The dedication service was held on April 28, with Ralph G. Cook as dedicatory speaker.

The group apparently felt that this new headquarters would be adequate for years to come. But by 1958 there was no more room for expansion. The adjoining building on the north was then purchased, and various departments moved into it, eventually occupying both the upper and lower floors.

---

[44] Minutes, 1949 General Conference.
[45] Ibid., 1950.
[46] Ibid., 1951.
[47] Ibid., 1952.

Second headquarters building of the United Pentecostal Church

God continued to bless the United Pentecostal Church numerically, and it soon became apparent that the group must build a suitable headquarters. The question was—where?

The following resolution had been adopted in the 1957 General Conference: "Since it is felt that the United Pentecostal Church would have a greater advantage in a smaller city, Be it Resolved, That the General Conference authorize the General Superintendent to appoint a committee to make a thorough investigation into the possibility of moving our headquarters to a smaller city." [48]

Carrying out this resolution, the committee had visited various smaller cities, but had found none that seemed suitable as a headquarters site.

Because of this, it was decided to keep headquarters in the St. Louis area. Accordingly, the General Board met in St. Louis on June 1, 1965, and authorized the purchase of an eight-acre tract of land in Collinsville, Illinois, nine miles from downtown St. Louis. Said General Superintendent Arthur T. Morgan: "Your headquarters will be located in the greater St. Louis area, enjoying the big city advantages, with a small town atmosphere." [49]

Later, there arose dissatisfaction with building in Collinsville. In the 1966 General Conference a resolution was introduced which, if it had passed, would have established headquarters in Little Rock, Arkansas. This resolution was defeated. [50]

A motion was then made that the General Board present to the conference its first, second and third choice for a headquarters city. The board retired to a private room, and soon brought back the following choices: first, St. Louis; second, Little Rock; and third, Tulsa. [51]

Seeing that it was unquestionably the will of the conference for headquarters to be located in St. Louis, officials began

[48] Ibid., 1957.
[49] Pentecostal Herald, September, 1965, p. 5.
[50] Minutes, 1966 General Conference.
[51] Ibid.

searching for a site in that city. The Building Committee, the Executive Board, and even the General Board examined various sites.

Finally, on April 16, 1968, the General Board decided upon an eight and one-half acre tract located at Dunn Road and Hazelcrest Drive in the north St. Louis suburb of Hazelwood.[52]

Ground was broken for the new building on December 20. 1968, with Mrs. Arthur T. Morgan, widow of the late beloved General Superintendent, turning the first shovel of dirt.[53]

Construction was begun early in 1969. The building was completed and occupied in the summer of 1970.

The impressive structure contains approximately 100,000 square feet of floor space.

The front section of the building has two stories. On the first floor there are departmental offices and a large, modern bookstore. The second floor contains offices, and a meeting room for the General Board.

In the center of the front section is a chapel with a ceiling two stories high. This chapel seats 200.

The rear part of the building will house a large, modern printing plant.

This commodious headquarters building, to be known as the World Evangelism Center, will enable the officials and staff to more efficiently serve the constituency of the United Pentecostal Church.

PUBLICATIONS

The Pentecostal Herald

Early Oneness Pentecostal organizations had few publications. Several years elapsed before any such organization began publishing even its own Sunday school literature. But there was one publication common to every Oneness group—

[52] Pentecostal Herald, May, 1968, p. 4.
[53] Ibid., February, 1969, p. 7.

Mrs. Arthur T. Morgan breaks ground for new headquarters building

Present headquarters building of the United Pentecostal Church

its official organ. This they considered an essential publication, looking to it to bind the members closer together as it publicized organizational activities, etc.

At the time of the 1945 merger, the Pentecostal Church, Incorporated published the Apostolic Herald, while the Pentecostal Assemblies of Jesus Christ published the Pentecostal Outlook. Taking the first half of one name, and the last half of the other, the merged body named its official organ the Pentecostal Herald.

The subject matter of this monthly periodical is slanted primarily to the ministers and laity of the organization, but there are articles beneficial to non-Pentecostals. The magazine also carries reports of organizational activities, as well as departmental publicity. In recent times, more space has been devoted to spiritual articles.

According to a resolution passed in the 1945 General Conference, the founding fathers had in mind a rather lenient editorial policy for the Pentecostal Herald. This resolution read: "Our official organ is the voice of the United Pentecostal Church, and its columns must be open to frank and courteous expression of opinion, even though such an expression may be contrary to the views of a portion of our members. Any committee or individual regulating the publication of such articles shall not be governed by doctrinal differences that are not contrary to our fundamentals of faith, but shall rule against only that which is written in the spirit of controversy." [54]

When articles of a questionable nature are received, the editor is to counsel with the Board of Publication, of which he is an ex-officio member. The decision of this board relative to such articles is final.[55]

Originally, the Pentecostal Herald was a sixteen-page periodical, but it was increased to twenty-four pages in February, 1954. From 1945 until 1954 the paper was printed in one color. From then until July, 1969 eight pages were printed

[54] Minutes, 1945 General Conference.
[55] Manual, 1970, p. 35.

in two colors. Beginning with the August, 1969 issue, the magazine was printed in two colors throughout. This has given it a far more attractive appearance.

Circulation has grown slowly but steadily. In 1970 approximately 25,000 copies were distributed monthly, with special issues reaching approximately 30,000.

The first editor of the Pentecostal Herald was M. J. Wolff, who was appointed by the Executive Board on November 9, 1945. At the same time, Paul H. Box was appointed Assistant Editor. He was to work in the office full time, while Wolff was to come in as occasion demanded.

Paul H. Box became editor in 1946, and served until his resignation in 1951. He was followed by Lester R. Thompson, who resigned in 1955. Arthur L. Clanton was appointed editor at the 1955 General Conference.

Sunday School Literature

In 1946 the United Pentecostal Church began publishing the following Sunday school quarterlies: Adult, Intermediate, Junior, Primary, and a teacher's quarterly for all age groups. These quarterlies were based upon the International Outlines.

It was soon felt, however, that these outlines tended to shy away from Biblical miracles, hence the organization obtained permission to use the outlines of the National Sunday School Association, beginning with the first quarter of 1948.

Publication of a Primary-Junior Teacher's Quarterly was begun in 1950. In the first quarter of 1952, these two quarterlies were separated, and the organization began publishing a Beginner-Primary Teacher's Quarterly.

A definite forward step was taken in 1961, when the group began publishing graded literature on the Beginner, Primary and Junior levels.

Another progressive move was made in January, 1969, when the name of the Intermediate Quarterly was changed to Junior-Hi, and a Junior-Hi Teacher's Quarterly was added.

Through these years, while the organization produced its own quarterlies, it continued to buy activity and visual aid materials from other publishers. These were often unsatisfactory, as they contained subject matter considered doctrinally unsound, or that did not measure up to the organization's standard of holiness.

Early in 1968 it was decided that something must be done to remedy this situation. General Superintendent Stanley W. Chambers appointed a Literature Survey Committee, headed by J. O. Wallace, General Sunday School Director, to determine the needs, and how they should be met. This committee met several times in the first half of 1968.

As an outgrowth of the committee's work, it was decided that the organization should formulate its own curricula for all age levels, and produce all its Sunday school literature, including activity and visual aid materials.

This literature, known as Word Aflame Publications, reached the classrooms for the October, 1969 quarter. At long last, the United Pentecostal Church had its own complete line of Sunday school materials.

Forward

This is the name of a twenty-eight page magazine, designed for only United Pentecostal ministers, which began publication in March, 1969. If fills a definite need of communication from headquarters to the ministry. And it falls behind in no detail when it comes to appearance and subject matter.

As to its contents, the magazine contains a full-length article directed to ministers, a report from the General Superintendent, sermon notes, departmental publicity (so designed that it can be separated from the magazine and given to the various local church departments), and other valuable helps for ministers.

J. R. Ensey was appointed editor of the magazine.

Forward is financed by the departments of the United

Pentecostal Church. Approximately 4,500 copies of each issue are mailed free to United Pentecostal ministers.

Books and Tracts

The publication of books has moved slowly in the United Pentecostal Church. Few books were published in the first twenty-five years. But in 1969 and 1970 plans were made to accelerate the book program.

The organization has been active in tract publication since its inception. But in 1968 it was felt that more should be done. A committee was appointed to completely evaluate all tracts, and take steps to upgrade the tract supply.

DEPARTMENTAL ORGANIZATION
FOREIGN MISSIONS

The importance attached to foreign missions by Oneness organizations is seen in this: following the formation of any organization, the first department created was that of foreign missions.

At the time of the merger of the Pentecostal Assemblies of Jesus Christ and the Pentecostal Church, Incorporated, both groups had foreign missionaries on the field. And, to a certain extent, the work of foreign missions had already been merged, for the two organizations were sharing in the support of at least nine missionaries.

Foreign Missions Policy

The first policy governing the Foreign Missions Department was the one formed by the harmonizing of the two manuals at the time of the merger in 1945.

The present policy is the result of years of experience and prayerful study. It deals with the sending of missionaries, their support, their conduct on the field, furloughs, mission schools, and various other essentials.

Foreign Missionaries and Their Fields

At the 1946 General Conference, seven new missionaries were appointed. This made a total of forty-seven missionaries under appointment supported by the United Pentecostal Church.[56]

By 1951 there were fifty active missionaries on the field, and four had recently been evacuated from China, making a total of fifty-four.[57] These missionaries were located in Alaska, Hawaii, Japan, Indonesia, Ceylon, India, South Africa, Liberia, Jamaica, Colombia, and Central America.

There were seventy-one missionaries in 1954, and these were located in sixteen fields. The four additional fields were Australia, Brazil, Uruguay and Nigeria.

Through the years, new fields have been opened, and additional missionaries sent. In November, 1969 the number of missionaries under appointment had grown to 112, and they were on, or scheduled to go to, the following twenty-nine fields: American Samoa, Argentina, Australia, Brazil, Chile, Colombia, Ecuador, England, Ethiopia, Germany, Ghana, Hawaii, Holland, India, Indonesia, Japan, Jamaica, Korea, Liberia, Madagascar, New Zealand, Nicaragua, Peru, Philippines, Puerto Rico, Rhodesia, South Africa, Uruguay, and Venezuela.

Missionary Finance

As the number of missionaries and mission fields increased, so did the offerings increase to meet the need. This growth is seen in the following figures: 1946, $79,506.29; 1950, $119,850.18; 1955, $188,566.61; 1960, $286,102.51; 1965, $419,066.27; and 1969, $759,683.08.

Foreign Missions Officials

When the United Pentecostal Church was formed in 1945,

---

[56] The Pentecostal Herald, December, 1946, p. 9.
[57] Ibid., November, 1951, p. 12.

Wynn T. Stairs was elected first Foreign Missionary Secretary. (This was the title then given the head of the department. In 1956, the title was changed to Director of Foreign Missions.) [58]

Wynn T. Stairs served as Director of Foreign Missions until his resignation in 1962, and Oscar Vouga was appointed to complete his unexpired term. Vouga was elected to the office in 1963, and served until 1969, when Tom Fred Tenney was elected to succeed him.

In the 1955 General Conference, Paul H. Box was appointed to serve as Foreign Missionary Office Secretary.[59] When the department head was designated as Director of Foreign Missions, a new office of Foreign Missionary Secretary was created, and Paul Box was appointed to fill this position in 1956.

Assisting the Director and Secretary is a Foreign Missionary Board of seven members.

A definite forward step was made by the department in 1968, with the forming of an office of Director of Promotions and Publications. Edwin E. Judd was chosen to fill this position, and began his duties in June of that year.

Partners in Missions

A bold new approach to the support of foreign missionaries, known as Partners in Missions, was instituted in 1969. The purpose of the program is set forth in these words: "It seeks to establish a direct personal link between missionaries abroad and saints at home. This personalized relationship will provide strength and encouragement in both directions. Missionaries will be sustained by the constant evidence of remembrance in the fellowship of faith and finance. Supporters at home will be stimulated to faithfulness in prayer and giving, as they identify themselves with specific needs of missionaries abroad on a continuing basis.

[58] Ibid., January, 1957, p. 8.
[59] Ibid., December, 1955, p. 19.

"An adequate budget is determined for each missionary under appointment. Before the missionary goes abroad, he, with the help of the Foreign Missionary Department, seeks those who will pledge to give a portion of this need each month that he is on the field. At least 20 churches or responsible individuals will share in the support of each missionary. Partnership shares may be in any amount from $10 per month on up to the suggested maximum for each missionary."[60]

With this plan, the department felt that it could better support the missionaries and the foreign missions cause.

Global Witness

This is the inspirational and informative monthly publication of the Foreign Missionary Department. It graphically presents the needs of the world, and the accomplishments of United Pentecostal Church missionaries. Edwin E. Judd is the editor.

HOME MISSIONS

From the beginning, the United Pentecostal Church has been interested in home missions. Each district sponsored the building of new works within its own boundaries.

But it was not until the 1952 General Conference that a General Home Missions Department was organized. The main purpose of this new department was to " . . . promote the evangelizing of states and territories not sufficiently covered by our organized districts."

Home Missions Policy

A reasonably comprehensive policy was adopted when the department was organized. It provided for a Home Missionary Secretary as head of the department. (In October, 1959 this title was changed to Director of Home Missions.)[61]

In addition, the department has a General Home Missions Board, made up of District Home Missions Directors; and a

---

[60] Ibid., January, 1970, p. 8.
[61] Minutes, 1959 General Conference.

General Home Missions Executive Committee, composed of the General Superintendent, the General Secretary, and the General Director of Home Missions. [62]

Home Missions Finance

To finance this department, twenty-five percent of all home missions offerings raised in the districts is to be sent each month to the General Home Missions Department.[63]

Before the forming of the General Home Missions Department, twenty-five percent of all undesignated foreign missionary offerings had been returned to the districts from which the offerings had come, to be used in home missions work in those districts. But with the forming of the general department, this practice was discontinued.[64]

Home Missions Officials

Stanley R. Hanby was elected first Home Missionary Secretary, in 1952. He resigned at the General Conference in 1957, and George L. Glass, Sr. was elected to replace him. Glass served until 1958, and was succeeded by C. Haskell Yadon, who resigned in 1967. J. T. Pugh was appointed Director of Home Missions in February of that year, to finish Yadon's unexpired term. Pugh was elected to the office in the 1967 General Conference.

A new office of General Home Missions Secretary was created in 1969, and J. R. Ensey was appointed to fill the position. Ensey had served the department as Coordinator of the Evangelism Commission since 1967.

Truth in Action

This program, originated in 1959, was designed to assist in the building of new works.

"The financial policy of Truth in Action is simply that each member gives an offering of $5 per quarter. By this, a revolv-

---

[62] Manual, 1970, p. 69.
[63] Ibid., p. 73.
[64] The Pentecostal Herald, April, 1953, p. 11.

ing fund is created, from which both loans and grants are made for home missions purposes. These funds are administered under the direction of the Home Missions committees and the General Home Missions office." [65]

By 1960 there were 250 contributing to the plan. It has helped to build approximately 100 churches.

Christmas for Christ

The purpose behind this unique plan, set up in the latter part of 1966, is to build new churches in unchurched cities and areas.

"Each family is requested to give the money normally spent on Christmas cards, stamps, decorations, and gifts, to the evangelizing of new cities with the true message of Christmas — peace to the troubled hearts of mankind. Gifts may be given to small children; however, the amount of the gift may be reduced, and the remainder given *by the children* as their own personal gifts to Christ.

"A special service will be set aside close to Christmas, when the members of each family will bring their gifts to the altar, and together give them to the Lord of harvest. . . ." [66]

From this fund, Christmas for Christ home missionaries receive living expenses, assistance in moving to the field of labor, money to buy or rent church facilities, advertising expenses, support for evangelists, etc.

Christmas for Christ offerings have increased each year, as the following approximate figures reveal: 1966, $106,000; 1967, $123,000; 1968, $150,000; and 1969, $227,000.

By 1969, there were 68 home missionaries on the field, supported by Christmas for Christ funds. Thirty-four new churches had been established, 800-1,200 were in Sunday school each Sunday, more than 150 had been baptized in Jesus' name, and more than 125 had been filled with the Holy Ghost.

Christmas for Christ enables home missions ministers to

[65] Ibid., April, 1959, p. 16.
[66] Ibid., December, 1966, p. 22.

devote their full time to evangelism, thus their churches grow faster, and become self-supporting sooner.

Outreach

This is the name of the bimonthly publication of the Home Missions Department. The first issue was printed in January, 1966. The magazine is devoted to the various phases of home missions work. J. R. Ensey was appointed editor in 1966.

PENTECOSTAL CONQUERORS

The international youth group of the United Pentecostal Church became known as Pentecostal Conquerors in 1946.

When the organization was formed in 1945, no provision was made for a general youth department. A committee composed of David F. Gray, Eldredge E. Lewis and Aubrey W. Buie was appointed to formulate a program and policy to be presented to the General Board and to the 1946 General Conference. This program and policy was adopted virtually as presented.[67] It has gone through minor revisions at intervals, but still remains generally as first formulated.

General Conquerors Officials

David F. Gray became first General President of the Pentecostal Conquerors. When he resigned in 1948, he was succeeded by Richard S. Davis. Joseph O. Moore followed Davis in 1949, and when he resigned in 1951, Calvin L. Rigdon was chosen to fill the position. In the fall of 1961, Rigdon resigned, and Tom Fred Tenney was appointed by the Executive Board to complete his unexpired term. Tenney announced in the 1969 General Conference that he would no longer consider the position, and Kenneth F. Haney was elected.

The first General Secretary of the Conquerors was Aubrey W. Buie. Ruby Keyes was elected to the position in 1947. When she resigned in 1955, James L. Kilgore was chosen to

---

[67] Conquerors Tread, January, 1963, p. 3.

succeed her. In the 1961 General Conference he declined to continue as secretary, and was replaced by Cleveland M. Becton, who served until 1967, when he was elected General Secretary of the United Pentecostal Church. Becton was succeeded by Donald Deck.

In the 1957 General Conference it was voted to put the General President on the field full time.[68] This accelerated the growth of the youth work.

In 1966, a new office was created in the Conquerors Department—that of Director of Promotions and Publications. Donald W. Fisher was appointed to fill this position. He was later appointed editor of Word Aflame Publications, and Thomas M. Jackson succeeded him on October 1, 1968.

Governing Committees

The General Youth Committee is composed of the General President, General Conquerors Secretary, and the District Presidents. They assist the General President in all matters pertaining to general youth work.

The Executive Youth Committee is made up of the General President, General Conquerors Secretary, and one or more members of the General Youth Committee. They assist the General President when the General Youth Committee is not in session.

Sheaves for Christ

At the General Conference in 1951, the General Conquerors Committee proposed a program whereby the Pentecostal Conquerors would raise funds to buy a truck for Bill Drost, missionary in Colombia. A contest was arranged between the Eastern and Western Zones. By September, 1952, $2,500 was raised.

A committee was then appointed to draw up plans for an

---

[68] Minutes, 1957 General Conference.

annual fund-raising program. The name, "Sheaves for Christ," was suggested by General President Calvin Rigdon.[69]

A goal of $10,000 was set for 1953, but only $1,554.67 was raised. Undaunted, the leaders set the 1954 goal at $10,000, and raised $3,558.64 that year.

Plaques were offered for the first time in 1955, and the offerings totaled $8,073.28. Now the program was well established, and the amount would steadily increase each year. In 1956, it was $20,354.85; 1958, $62,584.86; 1960, $128,149.25; 1963, more than $213,000; 1965, $277,920.91; 1967, $455,776.31; and 1969, $555,411.12.[70]

Proceeds from Sheaves for Christ are used mainly to assist foreign and home missions causes. In addition, dormitories and tabernacles have been built on district campgrounds, a beautiful dormitory (Conquerors Hall) stands at Tupelo Children's Mansion, scholarships have been given to qualifying students to attend Bible schools, Harvestime radio program has been helped, thousands of tracts have been printed in foreign languages, plus other worthy enterprises.

The Conquerors Tread

The first issue of this youth magazine was printed in July, 1962. It was a quarterly publication, distributed by the youth department, and designed to appeal especially to youth. It became a monthly publication in January, 1967.

W. C. Parkey was the first editor; Larry Blake was associate editor. Donald Fisher followed Parkey as editor in 1966, and served until 1969, when Thomas M. Jackson became editor. Circulation of the Tread in 1970 was 11,000 monthly.

Youth Week

The first International Youth Week was held in April, 1961, with a week's services scheduled around the world. Since that time, the third week in February has been desig-

---
[69] Conquerors' Tread.
[70] Ibid.

nated as annual youth week. Usually a visiting minister is called in, and revival services, directed by youth and slanted toward youth, are conducted. Many young people have been saved and blessed in these services.

Other Activities

The Conquerors Department also sponsors regional and national youth conventions, annual district youth camps, caroling for Christ at Christmas time, an annual national Bible Quizzing program, and other youth-related activities.

SUNDAY SCHOOL DEPARTMENT

A lengthy Sunday school policy was adopted at the 1945 General Conference. But in the 1946 General Conference, this was passed: "Inasmuch as the Sunday school policy adopted at the General Conference in 1945 is unsatisfactory, Be it Resolved, That the Sunday school policy be annulled. Be it further Resolved, That a committee be appointed to revise said policy." [71] This policy was revised, and presented to the 1947 General Conference, where it was adopted.

General Sunday School Officials

The official head of the Sunday School Department was first known as the General Sunday School Secretary.[72] This was changed to General Sunday School Director in 1953.[73] In 1961 this official was placed on the field full time.[74]

E. E. McNatt was appointed first official head of the department in 1948. Then, in the 1949 General Conference, he was elected to the position. He resigned in 1954, and Paul H. Box was appointed to fill his unexpired term.[75] In the 1955 General Conference, McNatt was again elected Sunday School

---

[71] Minutes, 1946 General Conference.
[72] Pentecostal Herald, January, 1948, p. 11.
[73] Minutes, 1953 General Conference.
[74] Ibid., 1961.
[75] Pentecostal Herald, July, 1954, p. 17.

Director, and served until his resignation shortly before the 1958 General Conference. At that time, J. O. Wallace was appointed to succeed him. Wallace was elected to the position in the 1959 General Conference.

J. Roy Weidner was elected Sunday School Secretary in 1957, and served until 1961, when he was followed by Raymond P. Kloepper.

A new office of Director of Publications and Promotions was created in 1968, and Daniel L. Segraves accepted the position on March 12 of that year.

Departmental Organization

The General Sunday School Board is composed of the General Sunday School Director, General Sunday School Secretary, Manager of the Pentecostal Publishing House, Editor in Chief, and the District Sunday School Directors. This board meets at each General Conference and General Sunday School Convention, and transacts business of the Sunday School Department.

The Executive Sunday School Committee is made up of the General Sunday School Director, Secretary, Manager of the Publishing House, Editor in Chief, and General Secretary. It handles departmental business between meetings of the General Sunday School Board.

Thirty Pieces of Silver

This annual fund-raising program of the Sunday School Department was adopted in 1960, and first publicized in January, 1961.[76] At first, plastic bags were distributed by the Sunday School Department to local Sunday Schools, which, in turn, gave them to the students. Later, envelopes and coin folders were used. On Easter Sunday these containers were brought in to the local Sunday schools, the money counted, and given as a "Thirty Pieces of Silver" offering.

---

[76] Pentecostal Herald, January, 1961, p. 11.

The theme of the drive was "Turn the price of betrayal into an offering of love."

Originally, 70% of this offering was retained by the local churches, 30% was sent to the District Sunday School Departments, and 50% of this amount was sent to the General Sunday School Department. In 1969 it was decided to divide the 1970 offering between the General and District Sunday School Departments, giving each 50%.

The 1969 offering totaled more than $110,000.

Fall Attendance Drive

The Sunday School Department originated its fall attendance program in 1962, and called it "One Million Contacts." Members of the Sunday schools were encouraged to make one million contacts, seeking to greatly increase Sunday school attendance.

More than seven million pieces of literature were distributed in this program between 1962 and 1965.

The program was called "Project Space Race" in 1966. From 1967 through 1970 it was known as "World-Wide Thrust."

Other Activities

The Sunday School Department worked long and hard to bring about the transition to graded Sunday school literature, first published in 1961. It worked even harder toward the organization's creating its own Sunday school curricula, and publishing its own visual aids and activity materials, a goal which was reached in October, 1969.

The department has been extremely active in promoting Teacher Training programs, and has sponsored several textbooks to aid in these programs.

Two of the more recent programs of the department have been Center of Interest teaching for Beginner through Junior classes, and Team Teaching for Junior Hi's and Senior Hi's.

Thrust

This quarterly periodical of the Sunday School Department was first published in October, 1968. It superseded the Sunday School Guide, which had been published since 1963. Thrust is devoted strictly to the building and operating of better Sunday schools. Daniel L. Segraves was appointed editor in 1968.

LADIES AUXILIARY

From the formation of the United Pentecostal Church, its faithful women labored in God's work in local church assemblies. But it was not until the organization was five years old that steps were taken to create a national Ladies Auxiliary.

In the 1950 General Conference, this was passed: "Inasmuch as many of our churches have a women's auxiliary ... helping in missionary work and other needs, Be it Resolved, That we have a (national) Ladies Auxiliary." [77] A committee was appointed to formulate a policy to be presented to the 1951 General Conference.

No policy was presented to this conference, however, and little was done in 1951, other than to decide on a national name—Ladies Pentecostal Auxiliary.[78] *(Note: In the 1953 General Conference, the name was changed to Ladies Auxiliary.)*

In the 1952 General Conference, another committee was appointed to organize the Ladies Auxiliary on a national scale.[79] This committee presented a Ladies Auxiliary policy to the 1953 General Conference, and the policy was adopted.[80] It included officers and their duties, district organization and government, and a financial plan.

[77] Minutes, 1950 General Conference.
[78] Ibid., 1951.
[79] Ibid., 1952.
[80] Ibid., 1953.

Ladies Auxiliary Officials

In 1954, the Executive Board appointed Mary Cole as the first Ladies Auxiliary President.[81] Lona Thames was appointed Ladies Auxiliary Secretary at the same time.

When Mary Cole resigned in 1960, Ila Ashcraft was appointed to the office. She died February 15, 1964, and was replaced by Vera Kinzie.

Lona Thames served as Secretary until her resignation in 1961. Florence Ripley was appointed as her successor, and held the office until 1965, when she was succeeded by Melissa Anderson.

In the beginning, the term of office in the Ladies Auxiliary was one year. This was changed to two years in 1968.

Mothers' Memorial

This annual fund-raising program was created in 1955. In 1956, the Mothers' Memorial offering was a modest $4,930.63.[82] But from this humble beginning, the annual drive gained momentum, and the total increased year by year. The following figures reflect this growth:

1957	$ 5,045.62
1958	8,530.86
1960	11,913.41
1963	18,438.55
1965	34,322.79
1967	84,889.86
1969	123,478.91

From the Mothers' Memorial fund, the Ladies Auxiliary has helped *foreign missions* — furnishing refrigerators, washers, dryers, stoves, foreign language tracts, etc.; *home missions* — giving a Mobile Evangelism Unit for use in new fields; *Harvestime* — sponsoring the program in Alaska, the Philip-

---

[81] Pentecostal Herald, July, 1954, p. 16.
[82] Ibid., May, 1957, p. 2.

pines, and Puerto Rico; *Tupelo Children's Mansion* — purchasing a new station wagon, and furniture for a new building; and *Bible schools* — donating library equipment.

Fifty percent of all Mothers' Memorial offerings remains in the districts where the offerings are taken.

Adopted Missionary Program

In 1967, the Ladies Auxiliary voted to "adopt" all United Pentecostal foreign missionary families. At Christmas time, each missionary couple receives $100, plus $10 for each child. Then, throughout the year, each missionary child is given $10, and sent an appropriate card, on his birthday.

EDITORIAL DEPARTMENT

The Editorial Department of the United Pentecostal Church was established in the 1946 General Conference.

Editorial Department Policy

The original policy governing this department was quite simple, containing only six main statements, one of which was followed by five secondary paragraphs.[83] The policy stated that the editing of all publications of the organization was to be placed in the hands of the Editorial Department. Specifically, the policy spoke only of the Pentecostal Herald (official organ) and Sunday school literature, since these were the only regular publications.

This first policy continued in the Manual through 1970, though many situations not covered by it arose, and were dealt with beyond the confines of the policy. A new Editorial Department Policy, far more comprehensive, was introduced in 1970.

Editorial Department Personnel

For approximately the first twenty years of the organization's history, all editorial work was done by one person,

---

[83] Manual, 1970, p. 49.

designated as the Editor of the Pentecostal Herald. But the work finally grew to such proportions that it was more than one could do. Consequently, the following was passed by the Executive Board in June, 1968:

> WHEREAS, There has been quite an increase in the work of the Editorial Department within the past few years; and
>
> WHEREAS, Much additional work is planned for this department, due to the proposed increase in Sunday school materials; be it therefore,
>
> *Resolved,* That the Executive Board appoint an editor for all Sunday school materials.
>
> The Editor in Chief (a new designation) shall continue to edit the Pentecostal Herald, books, tracts, and all other materials not classified in the preceding paragraph. He shall also serve as Editor in Chief of all Sunday school materials, scanning them for content only.[84]

Arthur L. Clanton, Herald editor, was elevated to the position of Editor in Chief. Donald W. Fisher was appointed by the Executive Board to serve as editor of all Sunday school materials.

Board of Publication

This board consists of the Editor in Chief (ex-officio), and three other members. It is the duty of the board to pass upon any publication or article of questionable nature.[85] Further, the Pentecostal Publishing House is to publish for the organization only those books and tracts approved by the Board of Publication.[86]

Departmental Publications

Publications of the various departments are not strictly

---

[84] Minutes, Executive Board, June, 1968.
[85] Manual, 1970, p. 40.
[86] Ibid., p. 50.

under the supervision of the Editorial Department, although the Editor in Chief does have the responsibility of finally passing upon such publications. Departmental editors of these publications are not members of the Editorial Department, as these editors have other duties in connection with their departments.

PENTECOSTAL PUBLISHING HOUSE

"There shall be a publishing house in St. Louis, Missouri, to be called the Pentecostal Publishing House." Thus is this vital Department of the United Pentecostal Church introduced.[87]

In 1944, the Pentecostal Church, Incorporated had bought property at 3449 South Grand in St. Louis, and had established the Pentecostal Publishing House. At the time of the merger in 1945, the United Pentecostal Church took over this publishing house, and continued its operation.

Purpose

According to the Manual of the United Pentecostal Church, the object of the Pentecostal Publishing House is ". . . to advance the cause of Christianity by disseminating religious knowledge, useful literature, and spiritual information, in the form of books, tracts, and periodicals." [88]

Publishing House Managers

The Manager of the Pentecostal Publishing House is appointed by the General Board, and his appointment is ratified by the General Conference.

T. R. Dungan, first manager, was appointed during the 1945 General Conference. [89] Dungan's resignation was presented to the Executive Board in its January 2, 1952 meeting,

---

[87] Ibid.
[88] Ibid.
[89] Minutes, 1945 General Conference.

and was accepted. In this same meeting, J. O. Wallace was appointed manager.[90] Wallace was re-appointed at the 1953 General Conference, but resigned shortly therafter. Ray Agnew was appointed to replace him, and became manager on November 1, 1953.[91]

Due to the heavy work load, David Schroeder was appointed Assistant Publishing House Manager in 1969. He had been unofficially serving in this capacity since October 7, 1968.

Growth

Sales and profits of the publishing house were relatively small in its early days. In the 1948 General Conference a resolution was adopted recommending ". . . that each district loan the Pentecostal Publishing House $100 for a period of three years, to be used as an operating capital."[92] There is no record that these loans were ever made.

Since that time, the publishing house has prospered. Instead of needing funds, it has been able to contribute thousands of dollars to the operation of the general headquarters. The following sales figures reflect publishing house growth:

1951	$107,915.41
1953	131,760.01
1955	177,499.48
1957	216,610.99
1960	256,204.51
1963	344,724.82
1966	426,024.92
1969	574,252.10

Printing Division

From 1945 until 1957, the Pentecostal Publishing House farmed out all its printing.

[90] Minutes, Executive Board Meeting, January, 1952.
[91] Pentecostal Herald, January, 1954, p. 16.
[92] Minutes, 1948 General Conference.

In 1957, the organization purchased printing equipment, and began doing its own printing. This original equipment consisted of a used 28×41 Miller flatbed letter press, a small vertical press, a hand-fed stitcher, a 42" longknife cutter, a 25×38 Baumfolder, and a few other pieces.

Added later were a Miller two-color or perfector offset press; a three-knife book trimmer; an automatic collator, stitcher and trimmer; equipment for a camera and layout department; ATF photo typesetting equipment, etc.

The first issue of the Pentecostal Herald printed by the publishing house was that of September, 1957. For the fourth quarter of that year, six Sunday school quarterlies were printed "inside," and by the first quarter of 1958, the publishing house was printing all its quarterlies.

The following sales figures show the growth of the Printing Division:

1957	$ 2,339.65
1958	50,392.74
1960	83,617.81
1963	107,652.54
1966	147,036.42
1969	243,268.69

With the advent of the new Sunday school literature program in 1969, it again became necessary to farm out some of the printing. Plans were discussed in 1970 to add the equipment necessary to bring all the printing back into the Pentecostal Publishing House.

HARVESTIME

From the early days of the United Pentecostal Church, many dreamed of having a national radio program. But several years elapsed before the dream became a reality.

The First Steps

In the 1952 General Conference, a resolution was adopted authorizing the appointing of a committee to investigate the possibility of having a national radio program. This committee was to report its findings at the 1953 General Conference.[93]

The committee reported at the 1953 conference, and its report was accepted.[94] Nothing further was done at that time.

Beginning of the Program

It was not until 1959 that definite steps were taken to get the program underway. The General Conference then authorized the Executive Board to do anything necessary to produce the program.[95]

A contest was sponsored to select a name for the broadcast. Naomi Lewis of St. Louis won, with the suggested name: Harvestime.

A Radio Commission was selected in October, 1960, and the program was on its way.

Harvestime was presented during the 1960 General Conference. March 5, 1961 marked the first broadcast, aired over 33 stations. From that time, the program expanded steadily. In August, 1963 there were 91 stations; by 1965 there were 132; by January, 1969 there were approximately 250. In late 1969 the number climbed to 318. The program is heard on several foreign stations.

Offiicials and Personnel

In the beginning, Harvestime was a part of the Home Missions Department. It was made a separate department in 1967.

According to the Radio Department Policy, incorporated into the Manual in 1967, officials of the department are a Radio Director, a Program Director, and a Radio Commission which serves mainly in an advisory capacity.[96]

---

[93] Minutes, 1952 General Conference.
[94] Minutes, 1953 General Conference.
[95] Ibid., 1959.
[96] Manual, 1970, p. 90.

Radio Directors. C. H. Yadon was first Radio Director. When he resigned in 1967, James G. Lumpkin was appointed to the position. Lumpkin resigned in May, 1969, and was succeeded by F. L. McKenzie.

Program Director. From the first broadcast, Nathaniel A. Urshan has been both Program Director and speaker. He has been assisted by Hugh Rose as announcer, musicians and a choir from Calvary Tabernacle in Indianapolis, and variour singers from throughout the United Pentecostal Church fellowship.

Promotional Directors. First to serve in this capacity was William Connell. He was strictly a "field" man, and did not occupy an office at headquarters. He was followed by W. C. Parkey, who came to headquarters in December, 1963. When he resigned in 1965, James G. Lumpkin was given the position. F. L. McKenzie became Promotional Director in October, 1967, following the resignation of James Lumpkin.

Harvestime Home Visitor

Published quarterly, in behalf of Harvestime, this periodical was first issued in 1968. It contains promotional material for the radio program, radio messages, etc. F. L. McKenzie is the editor.

The theme of Harvestime is "Reaching the Nations with Bible Salvation."

DEPARTMENT OF EDUCATION

The United Pentecostal Church had no actual Department of Education until 1968.[97]

One should not assume from this, however, that the organization had not before been interested in Christian education. From its inception, it had evinced an interest in the proper education of its youth.

The minutes of the 1945 merger conference hold no record

---

[97] Minutes, 1968 General Conference.

of the adoption of a policy governing Christian education. Evidently, the first policy was the one formed by the harmonizing of the manuals of the two former organizations. The policy was revised in 1946, and again in 1954.

Board of Christian Education

This board, consisting of five members, was first appointed at the 1945 General Conference. It had jurisdiction over all endorsed Bible schools. Its members made annual inspections of these schools, checking classrooms, preparation and serving of meals, living quarters, teaching staff, and curriculum. They then made a report to the General Board at each General Conference.

The Board of Christian Education also passed upon all applications from schools seeking endorsement, and had authority to recommend the withdrawing of endorsement from any school.

Department of Education Policy

This new policy, adopted at the 1968 General Conference, superseded the much simpler one of the Board of Christian Education.

The policy calls for a Superintendent of Education (departmental head), and a Secretary of Education. These officials are ex-officio members of the Board of Education. Three other members, appointed by the General Board, make up the Board of Education. *(Note: In the new policy, the word "Christian" was dropped from the title of this board.)*

The policy sets forth the duties of its officials, designates two classes of organizational colleges (district and non-district), gives the purpose of the department, enumerates the privileges and responsibilities of schools, instructs new schools as to how to obtain endorsement, etc.

By 1970 it could be clearly seen that the organization was showing an increased interest in the field of education.

Department of Education Officials

M. H. Hansford was appointed Superintendent of Education in 1968; James P. Silvernale was appointed Secretary of Education.

Endorsed Bible Schools

From 1945 through 1970, the United Pentecostal Church has endorsed eleven Bible schools. Eight of these schools were still in operation in 1970.

Apostolic Bible Institute. This school, located in St. Paul, Minnesota, was founded in 1937 within the framework of the Pentecostal Assemblies of Jesus Christ. For a more detailed history of its beginning, see chapter seven, page 83. The school opened with 14 students, and a faculty of three. It was endorsed by the United Pentecostal Church in 1945. In 1970 it had an enrollment of 256, with eleven faculty members.

Apostolic College. Located in Tulsa, Oklahoma, this school was established in 1938 within the confines of the Pentecostal Assemblies of Jesus Christ. For its early history, see chapter seven, page 83. The school was endorsed by the United Pentecostal Church in 1945, but endorsement was later withdrawn.

Apostolic Missionary Institute. This is one of the organization's newer schools. Located in Picton, Ontario, Canada, it opened in 1965 with seven students and five faculty and staff members. It was endorsed in 1966. In 1970, it had an enrollment of 31, with a combined faculty and staff of five.

Conquerors Bible College. Portland, Oregon is the site of this school, which opened in 1953, with 24 students and six faculty and staff members. It was endorsed in 1954. The school had 112 students and a faculty and staff of eight in 1970.

Gateway College of Evangelism. This, the organization's newest school, located in Florissant, Missouri, and owned by the Missouri District, opened on September 15, 1968. Originally, it had 75 students, and a faculty and staff of 12. In

1970, there were 112 students, and a combined faculty and staff of 12.

Ohio Bible College. Founded in 1956, this school was first known as Young Men's Bible Institute, and was located at Massillon, Ohio. In 1964, the school became co-educational, moved to Akron, Ohio, and changed its name. It was endorsed in 1962. Originally, there were eight students, and a faculty of three. In 1970, there were 51 students, and twelve faculty members.

International Bible College. Located in San Antonio, Texas, this school was endorsed in 1946. Endorsement was later withdrawn when the school was charged with teaching "Latter Rain" doctrine.[98] (Note: For an explanation of this doctrine, see page 143 of this chapter.)

Pentecostal Bible Institute. This school was founded by the Pentecostal Church, Incorporated, and opened on October 12, 1945, with 35 students and five faculty members. It was endorsed by the United Pentecostal Church in 1945. The school is located in Tupelo, Mississippi. In 1970, there were 60 students, and six faculty members. For more concerning this school, see chapter eight, page 103.

Southern Bible and Vocational College. Later known as Southern Bible College, this school was also founded within the framework of the Pentecostal Assemblies of Jesus Christ (see chapter seven, page 84). In 1943 it moved from Rising Star, Texas to Milford, Texas. It was endorsed by the organization in 1945, but did not continue long thereafter.

Texas Bible College. The Texas District was given authority in 1962 to establish this school in Houston. It opened with an enrollment of 45, and a faculty of six. In 1970, there were 276 students, and a faculty of twelve.

Western Apostolic Bible College. This school was started in 1953, with twelve students, and four faculty members. It is located in Stockton, California. The school was endorsed in

---

[98] Minutes, 1951 General Conference.

1954. In 1970, the enrollment was 200, and the faculty numbered sixteen.

TUPELO CHILDREN'S MANSION

In the beginning, Tupelo Children's Mansion was the dream of one man: T. C. Montgomery, Atlanta, Georgia pastor. Late in 1950, he was impressed with the need for a Pentecostal orphanage, where children would not only be cared for, but would be taught true Pentecostal doctrine.

On April 24, 1951, he resigned his church to work full time in raising funds for the Mansion. During that year, he traveled extensively in Georgia, Florida, Mississippi and Louisiana. On these various trips, he slept in his car twenty-eight times, to conserve money. At times he cooked on a camp stove, and shaved by some stream. By early 1952, he had raised $37,000 in cash and pledges.

During 1952, he traveled in Texas, Illinois and Alabama, still raising funds.

Approximately twenty acres were purchased near Tupelo, Mississippi in 1951. Construction was begun on the first building, and completed, in 1952. Since that time, five other buildings have been added.

The Mansion was officially endorsed by the organization at its 1952 General Conference.

In December, 1953 the first children, four orphaned girls, arrived at the Mansion. In 1969, sixty-three children lived there. During the intervening years, the Mansion provided a home for 130 children.

The children are kept, not only through high school, but until they get settled in life—in college, in service, in marriage, etc. They are financed through the first year in college or trade school, and may then borrow from a Mansion fund, if necessary, to complete their education.

L. J. Hosch, United Pentecostal minister (now deceased), served as Superintendent of the Mansion from November, 1953 until March, 1955. R. P. Kloepper, another United Pente-

1970 General Board of the United Pentecostal Church

costal minister, became Superintendent in April, 1955, and served until June, 1970. He was followed by Brian Chelette.

ORGANIZATIONAL GROWTH

In the first paragraph of this chapter it was stated that, in the beginning, there were 1,838 ministers and approximately 900 churches in the United Pentecostal Church.

On May 15, 1946, the Full Gospel Pentecostal Church of Canada voted to merge with the United Pentecostal Church. New Brunswick, Nova Scotia and Prince Edward Island made up the Maritime District.[99] This merger added a goodly number of ministers.

By January, 1953, there were approximately 2,800 ministers, according to a statement by General Superintendent Arthur T. Morgan.[100]

The 1969–70 Ministerial Directory showed 4,347 ministers, and 2,225 churches. This does not include ministers or churches in foreign missionary fields.

While the number of ministers and churches has increased more than two and one-half times, the number of laymen has correspondingly increased. No record is available, however, as to the number of laymen in the United Pentecostal Church, neither at its beginning, nor up until 1970.

---

[99] Pentecostal Herald, July, 1946, p. 4.
[100] Ibid., January, 1953, p. 7.

12
Profiles in Pentecost

This chapter was written with a feeling of hesitancy actually bordering on reluctance.

The reason? The biographies of many worthy Pentecostal ministers could not be included, due either to limited space or to the unavailability of information.

It was essential that these profiles be limited to ministers mentioned in the book. And not even all these could be included. The list had to be narrowed to include only those who were instrumental in forming the various organizations, or who held general offices in them. Additional information concerning these ministers will be found elsewhere in the book.

In future editions, perhaps other biographies can be added to these.

HOWARD A. GOSS

Howard A. Goss was born near Steelville, Missouri, March 6, 1883. He was the fifth of seven sons born to Clinton and Margaret Goss, who had moved to Missouri from Tennessee.

His early childhood was spent on a farm, and the forests around the homestead abounded in wild game.

In his book, "The Winds of God," Howard Goss says this about his childhood years: "Books we had, but no shoes. They had to be hand made in our locality. Only the older boys had shoes bought for them. I was about twelve years old when I had my first pair . . .

"We all worked from the peep of day until the darkness had settled down. Christmas and the Fourth of July were our only holidays . . .

"We had no feeling about lacking what today would be called the comforts of life, because life seemed full to us, and complete...."

In 1898, Clinton Goss sold the farm and moved to Galena, Kansas, where a boom was surging in the lead and zinc mines.

Howard Goss was converted in Galena, Kansas in 1902, under the ministry of Charles F. Parham. Soon afterward, he began to feel a call to the ministry. In 1905 he sold all his belongings, and went with a group of twenty-two workers to Houston, Texas.

In 1906, a band of workers in Houston boarded a train for a revival in another city. As they traveled, and worshipped God, He began to pour out His Spirit. It was at this time that Howard Goss received the Holy Ghost. During that same year he was ordained.

On February 24, 1907, he married Millicent McClendon, a well-known evangelist at that time. She died in 1910. In the fall of 1911, he was married to Ethel Wright, who died December 3, 1963. They were the parents of six children — three boys and three girls.

In 1912, he took his gospel tent to Hot Springs, Arkansas, and then settled there as pastor. In the fall of 1913, he rented the Grand Opera House and moved his congregation into it.

In November of that year, together with E. N. Bell, he issued an invitation to hold a convention in order to organize the Pentecostal work. E. N. Bell was elected Chairman; Howard Goss, Secretary. Out of this meeting came the organization known as the Assemblies of God.

It was about this time that the truth of baptism in the name of Jesus and of the Oneness of God was revealed. Howard Goss, along with many other ministers, accepted this truth.

In 1919 he moved to Canada, where he was instrumental in organizing the Pentecostal Assemblies of Canada, originally a Jesus' name movement. In 1920 he founded Bethel Pentecostal Tabernacle in Toronto. He pastored this church until 1937.

In 1939 Howard Goss returned to the United States, and was elected General Superintendent of the Pentecostal Church, Incorporated.

In 1945, he was elected the first General Superintendent of the United Pentecostal Church, and held this position until 1951.

Following this, he labored as a Bible teacher and spiritual adviser. He was active in the work of God until illness prevented.

Howard A. Goss' long and useful life in the service of God came to an end on July 13, 1964, at his home in Windsor, Ontario, Canada.

ARTHUR THEODORE MORGAN

Arthur T. Morgan was born August 27, 1901 in Lufkin, Texas, the only child of Joseph and Mary Morgan.

In 1907 the Morgans moved to Cravens, Louisiana, where young Arthur attended his first school. In 1916 they moved to Pinewood, Louisiana, and he attended the Rosepine school. He finished high school in De Ridder, Louisiana in 1918.

The Morgan family had in mind that their young son become a Doctor of Medicine, consequently they sought to enter him in the School of Medicine in New Orleans. But the high schools had not provided enough credits in Latin, needed for enrollment in medicine, so he was not accepted. (In retrospect, one can see the hand of God in this.) He later matriculated at Centenary College in Shreveport, Louisiana, and was there until called home to help with the work of his parents' farm and store.

On August 4, 1922 he was united in marriage to Nell Knight in De Ridder. They were blessed with four children.

The elder Morgans, who at this time were operating a farm and dairy, turned it over to the young couple. They operated the dairy until 1926, when Arthur Morgan entered Civil Service at the De Ridder Post Office. He continued in this position until 1932.

To regress somewhat, Oliver F. Fauss had conducted a revival meeting in 1916 in the area where the Morgans lived. The sermons had a lasting effect upon the entire family, and played a great part in their later receiving the Pentecostal experience. They asked Fauss for "chapter and verse" to prove his "strange" doctrine, and studied these scriptures intently. It was in this revival that Arthur T. Morgan heard the Pentecostal message for the first time.

About three and one-half years later, the young man found himself under conviction, began seeking the Lord, and received the Holy Ghost two weeks later.

During the years that he worked at the Post Office, he began to feel the call to preach. As all young preachers, he spoke where he could find an opening, developing his ministry so effectively that, in 1929, he was ordained, and affiliated with the Pentecostal Assemblies of the World. Later he became associated with the Pentecostal Ministerial Alliance.

In 1931 he was chosen pastor of the First Pentecostal Church of De Ridder, Louisiana, and held this pastorate for nearly two years.

In 1932, the Morgans moved to Alexandria, Louisiana, accepted the pastorate of a small, struggling work, and built it up into a flourishing church.

The twelve years in Alexandria were ended when he moved back to De Ridder in 1944, and became Assistant Postmaster. At this time he was also serving as District Superintendent of the South Central District of the Pentecostal Church, Incorporated.

In 1945, Arthur Morgan was called to the pastorate of Faith Tabernacle in Port Arthur, Texas. He gave up all civil service work, and devoted his full time to pastoring the church and to district work.

At this time, by virtue of office, he served with the General Board of the Pentecostal Church, Incorporated in its meetings with the General Board of the Pentecostal Assemblies of Jesus

Christ to consider the possibility of uniting these two larger bodies of Oneness Pentecostal people.

After the merger, he was chosen to serve as District Secretary-Treasurer of the Texas District. He also served as Chairman of the Board of Christian Education, and as a member of the Foreign Missionary Board.

In 1951, Arthur T. Morgan was chosen to fill the highest office in the United Pentecostal Church—that of General Superintendent. In this office, God signally blessed him. The United Pentecostal Church enjoyed phenomenal growth during his tenure of sixteen years.

He died suddenly while presiding over a General Board meeting in Tulsa, Oklahoma, on October 18, 1967.

WILLIAM THOMAS WITHERSPOON

W. T. Witherspoon was born at Wampum, Pennsylvania, on August 7, 1880. His early years were spent near his birthplace.

Later he moved to Pittsburgh, where he was employed as a salesman for a large equipment firm. It was in this city that he met Julia Blanche Crane, and they were united in marriage on September 10, 1902. They continued to reside in Pittsburgh for more than twelve years.

The Witherspoons were prominent in church work, first in the Methodist Episcopal Church, and then in the Christian and Missionary Alliance.

In 1912, W. T. Witherspoon received the baptism of the Holy Ghost. Three years later, God revealed to him the truth of the Oneness of the Godhead, and baptism in Jesus' name.

In 1914, he had been transferred to Columbus, Ohio, and had been made district manager of the firm by which he was employed.

Shortly after this, he received a definite call to the ministry. In 1917, he organized a group of people into a small congregation, known as the Apostolic Gospel Church. Many were the disappointments, heartaches, and trials that accompanied the building of this church, but the efforts of W. T. Witherspoon, and those associated with him throughout the years of his ministry, caused it to grow into one of the largest Oneness assemblies in the world. Pastor Witherspoon continued to work in secular employment for seven years, not wishing to be a burden to the church.

His keen spiritual vision also led to the establishing of five branch churches in Ohio—West Jefferson, London, Ironton, Springfield, and Dayton.

W. T. Witherspoon was the first Foreign Missionary Chairman of the Pentecostal Assemblies of Jesus Christ. While in this office, he traveled extensively in the United States and Canada, and visited the Hawaiian Islands, Jamaica, Palestine, and many of the principal countries in Europe.

Following this, he was chosen General Chairman of the Pentecostal Assemblies of Jesus Christ, serving from 1938 until it merged with the Pentecostal Church, Incorporated in 1945, to form the United Pentecostal Church.

He worked hard to bring about the merger of these two organizations. And at the merger conference, he was elected Assistant General Superintendent, a position he held until his death.

It was in this same General Conference that he was married to Mrs. Jet Stallones, a well-known minister, teacher, and writer. His first wife had preceded him in death.

He died on October 27, 1947. Shortly before his death, when his religious activities had been greatly curtailed, he said, "I am having the time of my life." He meant that, though seriously ill, the Lord had grown even more precious to him.

The life and ministry of W. T. Witherspoon has made a lasting contribution to the world, and to Oneness Pentecostal people.

GLADSTONE THOMAS HAYWOOD

Another well-known Pentecostal pioneer was the talented and deeply spiritual G. T. Haywood. He was born on July 15,

1880 in Greencastle, Indiana. When he was three, his family moved to Indianapolis.

While still in high school, he discovered his talent for cartooning and sketching. After graduating, he worked for two newspapers, hoping to become a writer or professional cartoonist. When this did not materialize, he left the paper, and took a job in a foundry.

In February, 1908 he met a man named Otis Barber, who had just received the Holy Ghost. Hearing Barber's testimony, conviction gripped his soul, and he attended his first Pentecostal revival. That very night he received the baptism of the Holy Ghost.

In February, 1909, he started his first mission, in cooperation with thirteen saints, at 12th and Missouri Streets in Indianapolis. There, with the exception of a brief interval, he continued until 1913. His ministry was blessed of God, and his congregation outgrew the small building. A new building was then erected at 11th and Senate Streets. In 1924, the congregation moved again, this time to Christ Temple, a large, beautiful building that still stands on one of the busy thoroughfares of Indianapolis.

G. T. Haywood was General Secretary of the Pentecostal Assemblies of the World (see chapter three). While serving in this position, he traveled extensively, and was in constant demand as a Bible teacher. The charts he used in this ministry were drawn by him. He was also editor of the Christian Outlook, official voice of the Pentecostal Assemblies of the World. In addition, he published a monthly paper known as the Voice in the Wilderness.

He is perhaps best remembered for the inspiring hymns which God moved upon him to write. Who has not been deeply stirred by singing such hymns as *I See A Crimson Stream of Blood; Thank God for the Blood; Behold the Bridegroom Cometh; Coming As A Thief in the Night; etc.?*

G. T. Haywood died April 12, 1931, at the comparitively young age of fifty-one years.

ANDREW DAVID URSHAN

Andrew D. Urshan was born in Iran, in a village called Abadjaloo, on May 17, 1884. This village lay approximately 400 miles northwest of Mt. Ararat, where Noah's ark rested.

He was converted in his homeland in 1900. In 1902 he came to the United States, landing in Yonkers, New York. He began preaching the gospel in 1904, and remained faithful to his calling until his death—63 years later.

In 1906, in Chicago, he witnessed a new touch of God's sanctifying grace, and a fresh divine anointing that set him on fire to win lost souls. Then and there he began personal work among the Assyrian people, with marked success.

Two years later, in 1908, the Holy Ghost baptism fell upon their converts in an unexpected manner in the Upper Room in Moody Bible Institute. This led him to seek the Lord again, with a new determination to receive this heavenly outpouring of God's Spirit. On July 4, 1908 the Lord baptized him with the Holy Ghost, and he spoke with other tongues for several hours.

The Lord privileged Brother Urshan to preach not only in the United States and Canada, but also in the British Isles, Holland, Norway, Sweden, Russia, and Persia (now Iran). During his lifetime he wrote and published at least eight books, which were widely distributed. He retained only one copy of each book, though thousands were printed.

He was ordained in 1910 in Chicago by William Durham.

In 1917, Andrew Urshan was united in marriage with Mildred Harriet Hammergren. They were blessed with four children: Grace, Faith, Nathaniel, and Andrew II, who died in 1951.

It was also in 1917 that he began publication of a monthly periodical known as The Witness of God, which he continued until the time of his death. He printed, and gave away, more than one hundred thousand tracts. In addition, he wrote many fine songs, both in English and in Aramaic. Perhaps one of his best-known songs was *There Is Sunshine in the Shadows*.

On November 29, 1932 he affiliated with the Pentecostal Assemblies of Jesus Christ, and served as a Presbyter in the Eastern States. During his many years as a minister, he effectively evangelized throughout the nation and the world. Thousands were won to the Jesus' name message through his fervent, earnest, prayerful ministry.

In 1933, he became pastor of the Satisfaction Gospel Mission (later the Apostolic Faith Christian Church) in New York City. He resigned this pastorate in 1950, and spent the remainder of his life speaking in special meetings, evangelistic services and conferences.

In the early 1950's Brother Urshan married Ethel May Dugas, who was his companion until death separated them. It was also in the early 1950's that he moved to Long Beach, California, which was his home until his death.

He preached his last message on October 12, 1967 in Bay City, Texas, in Pastor R. E. Johnson's assembly.

The inspiring and effective ministry of Andrew D. Urshan, the "Persian Evangelist," made a lasting contribution to the present-day Oneness Pentecostal movement as we know it. He was a strong preacher of the name of Jesus, and a lover of the message of holiness unto the Lord.

Andrew D. Urshan went to be with Jesus on October 16, 1967 in Bay City, Texas, at the age of eighty-two years, and five months.

His last words to his son were, "You go to the National Conference in Tulsa; I'm going to the International Conference in the New Jerusalem."

OLIVER F. FAUSS

Oliver F. Fauss was born May 22, 1898 on a farm in northwestern Oklahoma. He states in his book, "What God Hath Wrought," that their home there was built, by his mother's request, like a long hall. The rooms were made by curtains stretched on a wooden frame, so they could be easily moved out for a dance.

Oliver F. Fauss' early life is partially pictured by these words: "It was past midnight at our home. I stood leaning against the wall of the house, crying with a terrible earache. This was the first time I can remember ever trying to pray. I looked up, and said, 'Oh, God, I wish they would hurry and go home,' They were having an old-fashioned country dance inside. I wanted them to go home so Mother could have time to notice me. Papa was always too clumsy with his feet to dance, so he just sat in the corner and took care of my sister and me, while Mother had herself a time on the dance floor."

When he was five or six, Oliver Fauss attended church for the first time. The occasion was a Methodist revival. It was during this meeting that his mother was converted. One night young Oliver had gone to sleep as the service progressed. He says, "All at once I was awakened by a noise such as I had never heard before. As I raised up and looked . . . I noticed my mother shouting all over the front of the church. She had gone to the altar and had 'prayed through' as they called it." His father was wonderfully converted in the same revival. From that time, their home was completely changed.

When Oliver was eleven or twelve, the family moved to southern Texas. There he was converted while praying alone out in a pasture. Of this event, he said later, "If I had known at that time about the wonderful baptism of the Holy Ghost, I believe I would have received my baptism on the spot."

It was in 1911 that Oliver Fauss received the baptism of the Holy Ghost. He felt definitely called to work for the Lord. He attended services at a mission hall in Houston, and worked in street meetings until 1915, when he was baptized in Jesus' name, and entered the ministry. He was ordained on August 6, 1917. The first nine years of his ministry were spent almost entirely on the evangelistic field in East Texas and Louisiana. He was pastor of the First Pentecostal Church of Port Arthur, Texas, from 1924 until 1928.

On July 10, 1916 he was united in marriage to Jewel E. Smith. They were blessed with three children.

In November, 1924 he was chosen editor of the Pentecostal Witness (later the Pentecostal Outlook), and served for four years. He served as Chairman of the Apostolic Church of Jesus Christ for two years (1929, 1930), and was a Presbyter in the Pentecostal Assemblies of Jesus Christ until the merger. He also held the office of Chairman of the South Central Council (Pentecostal Assemblies of Jesus Christ) from 1930 until 1935.

In 1929 he founded Bethel Gospel Tabernacle in Houston, Texas, and was its pastor for approximately forty years.

Oliver F. Fauss was elected Assistant General Superintendent of the United Pentecostal Church in 1947, a position he still held in 1970. His wise counsel on both the General and Executive Boards has always been appreciated.

In October, 1967, when General Superintendent Arthur T. Morgan died suddenly, Oliver Fauss was appointed by the General Board to serve the two remaining months of his term.

Oliver F. Fauss will long be remembered as one of the foremost leaders in Oneness Pentecostal organizations.

RALPH G. COOK

Ralph G. Cook was born September 1, 1899 in Boston, Massachusetts.

His first memories of God were in the Methodist Church, but he states that he never found any real satisfaction there, though he was sprinkled twice, once when he was a baby, and again when he was twelve years old. He did have a hunger for God, and attended services in the Nazarene Church, the Holiness Church, and the Salvation Army.

When Ralph Cook was sixteen, he heard the true gospel for the first time. God's messenger was the boy's uncle, who had been an alcoholic, but had been marvelously saved in California. This uncle took him to the Pentecostal Church in Chelsea, Massachusetts, where he attended for about a month, and was brought under deep conviction. He went to the altar in this church.

He gives this inspiring account of being filled with the Spirit:

"Two nights after I first went to the altar, I was sitting in a boarding house with two young men. They were instructing me in the way of the Lord, when suddenly the power of God fell on me, and I began to speak with other tongues as the Spirit gave utterance. It was about 9:00 o'clock at night, and I really stirred that boarding house. The landlady came down, and requested that I be taken out of there. They took me over to the church, and I was there until 3:00 o'clock. It was a wonderful experience!

"The church that I had been attending believed in three works of grace, and the pastor could not understand how I had received the Holy Ghost without first being sanctified. He stood over me for two hours, rebuking the Devil, but finally he reconciled himself to the fact that I had the genuine experience. Those were days of heaven on earth."

In 1917 Ralph Cook received the revelation of baptism in Jesus' name, and of the oneness of God. He went from a church of about four hundred members into a little church of about twenty-five members. This was at Hyde Park, Massachusetts.

While attending this church, he met and married Miss Hattie Lowell. They had been married about one year and two weeks when the dreadful scourge of influenza hit the country. His wife lived just three days after falling ill, and he had the sad experience of burying her and a premature baby together.

Ralph Cook felt the call to the ministry, and was ordained in Boston by N. Alexander. He went to Indianapolis in 1919, where he attended G. T. Haywood's church. Afterwards, he went to Bloomington, Indiana and pastored a small group. This church was on Sixteenth Street, at the same spot where the Pentecostal Assembly church now stands. During his ministry there, the church was blessed with a fine revival, and many received the Holy Ghost.

Leaving Bloomington, he traveled through Indiana and Southern Illinois in evangelistic work. During this time, he met a young evangelist by the name of Nellie Reppond, and they were married July 3, 1920.

His next pastorate was in Carrolton, Illinois. Following that, he went to Louisiana, and then to Hot Springs, Arkansas, where he assisted H. E. Reed for seven months.

In 1921, he became pastor of the church in Little Rock, Arkansas, and remained there for about three years. He resigned the pastorate in 1923, turning the work over to the late G. H. Brown, who had been assisting him.

He founded the church in Foxboro, Massachusetts, and served as pastor for twenty-one years.

He accepted the pastorate of the First Apostolic Church in Lancaster, Ohio in 1945.

Ralph Cook has held several official positions. He was a District Elder in the Pentecostal Assemblies of the World. He was a member of the Apostolic Church of Jesus Christ, and later became affiliated with the Pentecostal Assemblies of Jesus Christ. In 1938, he was chosen to serve on the General Board of that organization, and held that position until the merger in 1945. He was then elected District Superintendent of the Ohio District (United Pentecostal Church), and served until 1954. For approximately nine years he was a member of the Foreign Missionary Board. In 1963 he was elected Assistant General Superintendent of the United Pentecostal Church.

OSCAR VOUGA

Oscar Vouga was born June 29, 1903 in St. Louis County, the fourth of ten children.

The spiritual turning point in his life came in 1924, when he was filled with the Holy Ghost and baptized in Jesus' name in Oakland, California, at the Big Downtown Mission, under the ministry of Pastor Harry Morse.

That same year he married. In December of that year he

was ordained, and he and Sister Vouga went to Hawaii as missionaries on December 27. They remained in Hawaii until 1932, with the exception of approximately one year spent in the states in the years 1926 and 1927.

He affiliated with the Pentecostal Ministerial Alliance in 1930.

Oscar Vouga has held several successful pastorates. His first, after returning from Hawaii, was in Nampa, Idaho, where he labored until 1935. At that time, he accepted the church on 78th and E Streets in Houston, Texas, remaining there until 1937. In 1937 and 1938, he served as pastor of the church in Bemis, Tennessee. From 1941 until 1943, he was pastor of Apostolic Temple in Winnipeg, Canada. Following the merger conference in 1945, he returned to Winnipeg and established Bethel Tabernacle, the first United Pentecostal church in that part of Canada. He pastored in Prichard, Alabama from August, 1953, until January 1, 1963.

Before the merger, he was a member of the Pentecostal Church, Incorporated, and served this organization in various capacities. While attending his first General Conference in 1932, he was appointed a member of the Foreign Missionary Board. In December, 1943, he was appointed editor of the Apostolic Herald. Then, in January 1944, he became Assistant General Secretary, and when the late Harry Branding resigned a few months later, he became General Secretary. At the General Conference in 1944, he was appointed manager of the newly-formed Pentecostal Publishing House, while continuing his duties as General Secretary and editor.

The name Oscar Vouga figures prominently in the account of the merger in 1945. When committees were appointed from the Pentecostal Church, Incorporated and the Pentecostal Assemblies of Jesus Christ, to work out terms of the merger, he served as secretary of the two joint meetings. When the two General Boards met jointly later that year, he again served as secretary. Following this, he was appointed secretary for the combined General Conference meetings.

In the merger conference he stepped down from office, in order that officials could be selected from both the former organizations. At that time, he was appointed a member of the Foreign Missionary Board of the United Pentecostal Church, and held this position until 1949, when he was elected Assistant General Superintendent. He continued in this office until 1962, when he was chosen to fill the office of Director of Foreign Missions. He served faithfully and well in this office until October, 1969.

No history of Oneness Pentecost would be complete without including the ministerial activities of Oscar Vouga.

BENJAMIN HARRISON HITE

B. H. Hite was born September 2, 1888 in Franklin, Kentucky. One of seven children born to John and Emily Hite, he was destined to have a great part in the work of God.

His mother was laid to rest when he was only ten years of age. At her passing, she made a profound impression upon her young son by saying that she would not mind dying if she knew that he and his younger sister would grow up to serve the Lord.

B. H. Hite was united in marriage to Mary Vanover on December 26, 1911, at Nashville, Tennessee. To this union were born ten children.

In 1912, when he was still a young man, God began to deal with B. H. Hite. He was converted in a cottage prayer meeting. At this time he wholly accepted God as his healer, and threw away all his medicine.

A few days later, H. W. Coulon came to Nashville, preaching the message of the baptism of the Holy Ghost. B. H. Hite had never heard this message, but when he did, he said that he wanted all that God had for him. In October, 1912, he received the Holy Ghost at a ladies prayer meeting, and spoke with tongues for about five hours. Shortly thereafter, he acknowledged his call to preach the gospel.

At the beginning of his ministry, he preached on street corners, in jails, in cottage prayer meetings – in fact, anywhere there was an open door. In his first cottage prayer meeting, a blind woman was divinely healed. (Surely this was, in a sense, prophetic of his future ministry, for many were divinely healed through the years, as he prayed for them.) He opened his first mission in 1913. But he soon felt the call to enter evangelistic work, and this led him into the mountain areas, as well as to many places in Tennessee, Arkansas, Oklahoma, Illinois, and Missouri. He founded missions which have grown into fine churches. In 1920, he opened a small mission in Granite City, Illinois. In 1923, he conducted services in Belleville, Illinois, and many received the Holy Ghost.

B. H. Hite's first ministerial affiliation was with the Assemblies of God. Then, in 1916, he received the light on baptism in Jesus' name, and affiliated with the Pentecostal Assemblies of the World. Later he became a member of the Pentecostal Church, Incorporated. From the time of the merger in 1945, until his death, he was a faithful member of the United Pentecostal Church.

He served also in various official positions. He was the first General Chairman of the Pentecostal Church, Incorporated, being elected in 1934, and serving until 1939. In this same organization, he later held the position of District Superintendent of the Central District, made up at that time of Illinois, Missouri and Kentucky. When Missouri separated from the Central District to form a district of its own, he became the District Superintendent. He continued to hold this position in the United Pentecostal Church until the time of his death.

B. H. Hite played a prominent part in helping to bring about the merger, in 1945, of the Pentecostal Church, Incorporated and the Pentecostal Assemblies of Jesus Christ.

In 1921, he came to St. Louis, Missouri to start a church. At the time he had two children. He came into the city with only three dollars. And on that same day he gave half of this to a needy fellow-minister. (Such was typical of him.) He had faith that God would take care of him, and He did. In St. Louis he established the First Pentecostal Church, and pastored it until his death, twenty-seven years later God mightily blessed his labors, and gave him many souls. From his church, approximately forty ministers went out into the work of God.

B. H. Hite was called home on May 23, 1948. He is gone, but the work he did lives on.

SAMUEL C. McCLAIN

Samuel McClain was born February 25, 1889 on a farm near Madison, Georgia.

From the time of childhood, he attended Sunday school, the younger children and his mother riding in a two-seated buggy, while the older children walked.

When he was about eight, he was asked what he planned to be when he became a man. He replied, "I am going to be a preacher."

When Sam McClain was fourteen, his parents moved to Arkansas. There, in an old-fashioned Baptist revival, where people shouted, and even fell under the power, quite a number of young people joined the church, he among them. Of this occasion, he said,

"I got nothing from God then, but a short time later, when reading the Bible, I raised my hand, looked toward heaven, and said, 'Jesus, I love You, and thank You for dying on the cross that I might be saved from sin, and go to heaven.' Oh the love and glory that exploded in my soul. I wanted to love Him, and do all that I could to please Him."

At the age of 16, he began teaching an Adult Sunday school class. At 17, he was called to preach, though he told no one of this call for a whole year. Instead of heeding the call, he attended a business college, and accepted a position to teach school.

At the end of the first school term, the "Apostolics" were granted permission to hold a revival in the school building. From the first night, Sam McClain was convinced that they had something he did not — something he wanted. On May 25, 1912 he received the baptism of the Holy Ghost. He described the experience in these words:

"It seemed that a barrel full of glory was charged with electricity, and poured over and through me. Suddenly it moved up and took hold of my mouth and tongue. Such words I had never spoken in all my life! I just listened, as the Holy Ghost talked through me."

After receiving the Holy Ghost, Sam McClain began to receive calls to conduct prayer meetings. The preaching of his first sermon grew out of rather amusing circumstances. A young man had arranged to conduct revival services. But when the time drew near, he developed "cold feet." He said, "Brother Sam, I just can't go; will you go for me?" Sam McClain did go, accompanied by John Alford. For some reason, he felt that John Alford was to do the preaching, and offered to pray for him. Alford replied, "Brother Sam, I never did preach in my life, and I don't have the Holy Ghost yet." So Sam McClain preached on "Behold the Lamb of God."

He was ordained on August 14, 1914. On January 16, 1916 he was baptized in the name of Jesus Christ.

As a gospel pioneer, conducting revivals in Arkansas, Kansas, Oklahoma, Texas, and New Mexico he established several churches. He and those assisting him know what it was to go hungry, and to be persecuted for the name and cause of Christ. His gospel tent was burned, one church had all the windows broken out, they were pelted with rocks and eggs, and once a stove was thrown through a window. His life was threatened. But none of these things moved him.

His ministry was diversified. He pastored churches in Ft. Smith, and Arkadelphia (Arkansas); El Paso, Amarillo, Canadian, Lubbock, and Le Feria (Texas); Albuquerque, New Mexico; Aberdeen, Mississippi; and Rupert, Idaho. He taught in D. C. O. Opperman's Bible School in Eureka Springs, Arkansas during 1918–1920, and in the Pentecostal Bible Institute, Tupelo, Mississippi, from 1947 until January, 1950. In addition, he served as Arkansas State Overseer in the Pentecostal Assemblies of the World from 1921 through 1925; was a District Presbyter for the Texas District of the Pentecostal Church, Incorporated in 1934 and 1935; and was District Secretary-Treasurer for the Arkansas District of the United Pentecostal Church during 1946. He was Editor of the Apostolic Herald, official voice of the Pentecostal Church, Incorporated, from 1937 until 1940.

He accepted the pastorate of the church in La Feria, Texas in 1964, and continued there until his retirement.

Samuel McClain passed on to his reward on February 24, 1969.

HARRY W. BRANDING

Harry W. Branding was born May 23, 1891, near Granite City, Illinois.

He received the baptism of the Holy Ghost in 1929, under the ministry of B. H. Hite, and began preaching a short time later. For thirty-four years he was pastor of Apostolic Pentecostal Church in St. Louis, Missouri, and saw it grow from a small congregation into one of the largest churches in the United Pentecostal Church.

From the beginning of his ministry, Harry Branding was active in organizational work. In 1943 he served as General Secretary of the Pentecostal Church, Incorporated. After the formation of the United Pentecostal Church, he was, for a time, a member of the Foreign Missionary Board, and of the Board of Christian Education. At the time of his death, on September 8, 1969, he was District Superintendent of the Missouri District, a position he had held since 1948; a member of the Board of Publication; a trustee of Tupelo Children's Mansion; and Chairman of Gateway College of Evangelism, which he had helped establish in 1968.

Epilogue

The Backward and Forward Look

The Apostle Peter, in his Second Epistle, spoke of stirring up our minds ". . . by way of remembrance." From the vantage point of the present, let us take

A Look at the Past

One who has read this book must realize that God has done glorious things for Oneness Pentecostals. Call to mind the time when there was no Oneness organization. Then visualize once more the humble beginning, when a mere handful of dedicated ministers met, and formed the first simple organization which, at that time, met their needs.

Follow the development of succeeding organizations, noting how each one grew more complex, with an ever-increasing number of faithful adherents, and with a constantly-growing ability to accomplish more for the cause of Christ.

Wend your way at last to the present, and see the inner workings of the mighty United Pentecostal Church, with its various inter-related departments, each one dedicated to the spreading of the true gospel.

Do this, and you will be compelled to exclaim, as did W. T. Witherspoon after the 1945 merger: "What hath God wrought!"

A Look into the Future

The Apostle Paul spoke of ". . . forgetting those things which are behind. . . ." There is no contradiction between his statement, and that of Peter's, quoted above. Paul simply meant that, so far as being satisfied with past accomplishments is concerned, we should forget the past, and look to the future.

And every department of the United Pentecostal Church is doing just this. There is no resting upon laurels, no complacent contentment with past achievements. Every eye is turned toward tomorrow.

New horizons of growth and accomplishment stretch out before us. Never-before-seen vistas of service thrill our hearts.

May God bless the United Pentecostal Church, as it walks with Him into the future.

INDEX

Agnew, Ray, 173
Anderson, Melissa, 169
Apostolic Bible Institute, 83, 178
Apostolic Church of Jesus Christ, 33, 36, 53, 62–69, 70, 107, 108, 110, 111, 112, 113, 114
Apostolic College, 83, 178
Apostolic Missionary Institute, 178
Ashcraft, Ila, 169
Assemblies of God, 18, 19, 21, 22, 23
Assistant General Superintendent, 131, 133

Baptism in Jesus' name
  Parham's statement, 13; Howard Goss baptized, 13, 14; revealed to A. D. Urshan, 14; generally revealed, 15; Frank Ewart begins preaching it, 16; E. N. Bell baptized, 18–21; others baptized, 18; Pentecostal Ministerial Alliance, 47; Pentecostal Assemblies of Jesus Christ, 80; Pentecostal Church, Incorporated, 98; United Pentecostal Church, 141, 142
Baptism of the Holy Ghost, 14, 18, 47, 79, 80, 98, 121, 141, 184, 186, 187, 189, 190, 192, 194, 195, 197, 200, 201
Basis of ministerial fellowship, 48
Becton, Cleveland M., 163
Bell, E. N., 18–21
Bible schools
  Apostolic Bible Institute, 83, 178; Apostolic College, 83, 178; Apostolic Missionary Institute, 178; Conquerors Bible College, 178; Gateway College of Evangelism, 178; Intermountain Christian Institute, 103; Northwest Bible and Training School, 103; Ohio Bible College, 179; Pentecostal Bible Institute, 103, 179; Pentecostal Bible Training School, 103; Southern Bible and Vocational College, 84; Texas Bible College, 179; Western Apostolic Bible College, 179, 180
Board of Christian Education, 104
Books, 156
Box, Paul H., 126, 154, 158, 165
Branding, Harry W., 95, 118, 201
Brickey, J. C., 34, 35, 41, 111

Chambers, Stanley W., 126, 133, 137
Church, entrance into, 24
Clanton, Arthur L., 103, 154, 171
Clibborn, Wm. E. Booth, 18, 30, 33
Cole, Mary, 169
Conquerors Bible College, 178
Cook, Glenn A., 16
Cook, Ralph G., 30, 133, 147, 193, 194
Crane, Clarence, 96

Deck, Donald E., 163
Department of Education
  Organized, 176, 177; officials, 178
District organization, 39–41, 65, 73–75, 93, 137–139
District Presbyters, 39, 74, 93, 94, 140
Doctrinal position
  Apostolic Church of Jesus Christ, 66; Pentecostal Assemblies of Jesus Christ, 79, 80; Pentecostal Church, Incorporated, 98, 99; Pentecostal Ministerial Alliance, 47, 48; United Pentecostal Church, 141–143
Dungan, T. R., 126, 172

Ecumenical movement, 146
Editorial Department, United Pentecostal Church, 170–172
Emmanuel's Church in Jesus Christ, 52–61, 62, 105, 106, 107
Ensey, J. R., 155, 160, 162
Ewart, Frank J., 15, 16, 17, 18
Executive Board, 37, 90, 134

Fauss, Oliver F., 19, 22, 27, 31, 64, 111, 118, 119, 121, 131, 133, 191, 192
Floyd, Lee, 23
Foreign missions
Organization, 25, 44, 55, 66, 77, 78, 96, 157–159; officials, 32, 44, 55, 66, 77, 78, 96, 158; publication (Global Witness), 159
Forward magazine, 155
Frush, James A., 41, 70, 77, 111, 113

Gateway College of Evangelism, 178
General Assembly of the Apostolic Assemblies, 23–26, 27
General Board, 37, 63, 72, 90, 133
General Conference, 36, 37, 51, 63, 71, 88, 130
General officials listed
General Assembly of the Apostolic Assemblies, 23; Pentecostal Assemblies of the World, 27; Pentecostal Ministerial Alliance, 41; Emmanuel's Church in Jesus Christ, 54; Apostolic Church of Jesus Christ, 64, 65; Pentecostal Assemblies of Jesus Christ, 75, 76; Pentecostal Church, Incorporated, 94, 95; United Pentecostal Church, 131, 132
General Secretary-treasurer, 65, 73, 92, 133
General Superintendent (Chairman), 39, 64, 72, 91, 131
Glass, George L. Sr., 160
Goss, Howard A., 13, 23, 33, 35, 41, 47, 48, 50, 94, 98, 107, 111, 119, 121, 123, 126, 128, 131, 137, 143, 183–185
Gray, David F., 162
Growth of organizations, 50, 58, 86, 104, 182
Gurley, A. D., 33, 100, 104, 109

Hall, L. C., 18, 41
Hanby, Stanley R., 76, 111, 119, 125
Haney, Kenneth F., 162
Hansford, M. H., 178
Harvestime
Organized, 174, 175; officials, 175, 176; publication (Harvest Home Visitor), 176
Hayes, Dan, 45, 56, 97
Haywood, G. T., 15, 16, 17, 27, 188, 189
Herald Publishing House, 99, 100
Hite, B. H., 94, 102, 119, 197, 198

Home missions
Forerunner, 96; organized, 159 to 162, officials, 160; publication (Outreach), 162
Hosch, L. J., 180
Hunter, A. D., 100

Interracial relationships, 27, 28, 31, 32, 33, 70, 84, 85, 86, 115

Keyes, Ruby, 162
Kidson, W. E., 33, 34, 41, 49, 50, 87, 95, 97, 99, 100, 101, 104
Kilgore, James, 162
Kinzie, Vera, 169
Kloepper, Raymond P., 166, 180

Ladies Auxiliary
Organized, 168; officials, 169; activities, 169, 170
LaFleur, Robert, 18
Latter Rain, 143, 144, 179
Lewis, Eldredge, 79
Lumpkin, James G., 176
Lyon, W. H., 41, 53, 54, 59, 106, 107

McAlister, R. E., 15
McClain, Samuel C., 13, 22, 27, 28, 29, 31, 100, 199–201
McKenzie, F. L., 176
McNatt, E. E., 165

Manner of election, 73, 92, 135, 136
Membership for local churches, 43, 75, 94, 140
Membership for ministers, 23, 42, 43, 54, 65, 76, 77, 95, 140
Mergers
General Assembly of the Apostolic Assemblies with Pentecostal Assemblies of the World, 27; Emmanuel's Church in Jesus Christ with Apostolic Churches of Jesus Christ, 59–61; Apostolic Church of Jesus Christ with Pentecostal Assemblies of the World, 68, 69; Pentecostal Assemblies of Jesus Christ with Pentecostal Church, Incorporated, 116–127
Mergers, unsuccessful attempts
Emmanuel's Church in Jesus Christ with Pentecostal Ministerial Alliance, 105–112; Pentecostal Assemblies of Jesus Christ with Pentecostal Church, Incorporated, 113–115

Ministerial lists
  General Assembly of the Apostolic Assemblies, 24, 25; Pentecostal Ministerial Alliance, 50, 51; Emmanuel's Church in Jesus Christ, 59; Apostolic Church of Jesus Christ, 67; Pentecostal Assemblies of Jesus Christ, 86; Pentecostal Church, Incorporated, 104; United Pentecostal Church, 182
Montgomery, T. C., 180
Moore, A. O., 96
Moore, Joseph, 162
Morgan, Arthur T., 131, 149, 185 to 187
Morgan, Mrs. Arthur T., 150
Morse, Harry, 15, 96
Mulford, W. M., 41, 46

Ohio Bible College, 179
Oneness, 13, 142
Oneness people not Unitarians, 143
Ooton, L. R., 41, 70, 75, 118
Opperman, D. C. O., 19, 21, 23

Parham, Charles, 13
Pentecostal Assemblies of Jesus Christ
  Formation, 68, 69; General Assembly, 71; General and Executive Boards, 72; General Chairman, 72; General Secretary, 73; manner of election, 73; district organization, 73–75; local churches, 75; general officials listed, 75; ministerial membership, 76, 77; foreign missions, 77; youth, 78; Sunday school, 79; doctrinal position, 79; publications, 80–82; headquarters, 82; Christian education, 83, 84; interracial relationships, 84, 85; growth, 86; 113, 114, 115, 117, 118, 119, 120, 121, 122, 124, 125, 126, 128, 129
Pentecostal Assemblies of the World, 27–34, 35, 54, 68, 69, 70, 71, 79, 82, 84, 86, 114, 115
Pentecostal Bible Institute, 103, 179
Pentecostal Church, Incorporated, 39, 86
  Name changed from Pentecostal Ministerial Alliance, 87; General Conference, 88; General and Executive Boards, 90; General Chairman (or Superintendent), 91; General Secretary, 92; manner of election, 92, 93; district organization, 93; local churches, 94; general officials listed, 94, 95; foreign missions, 96; Sunday school, 97; youth, 97; doctrinal position, 98; publications, 99–101, headquarters, 101, 102; Christian education, 102–104; growth, 104; 113, 114, 116, 117, 118, 119, 120, 121, 122, 123, 124, 125, 126, 128
Pentecostal Ministerial Alliance, 35–51, 52, 87, 88, 91, 105, 106, 107, 108, 109, 110, 111, 112, 113
Pentecostal Publishing House, 102, 172, 173
Periodicals (official organs)
  Blessed Truth, 13, 21; Pentecostal Witness, 31, 57, 61, 66, 67; Apostolic Herald, 48, 49, 100; Pentecostal Outlook, 81; Pentecostal Herald, 150, 153
Printing, 82, 101, 173, 174
Pugh, J. T., 160

Reed, T. Richard, 97
Remission of sins, 24
Repentance, 24
RSV Bible, 144
Rigdon, Calvin L., 162
Ripley, Florence, 169
Roberts, L. V., 19, 23
Rogers, H. G., 18, 19

Silvernale, James P., 178
Smith, Karl, 70, 75, 81, 82
Social gospel, 146
Southern Bible Conference, 29–31
Southern Bible and Vocational College, 84, 179
Stairs, Wynn T., 78, 126, 158
Standard of salvation, 24
Sunday school
  Organization, 45, 79, 97, 166; officials, 45, 56, 165, 166; literature, 32, 49, 57, 101, 154, 155; periodical (Thrust), 168; other activities, 166, 167

Tenney, Tom Fred, 158, 162
Texas Bible College, 179
Thames, Lona, 169
Tracts, 156
Tupelo Children's Mansion, 180, 182

United Pentecostal Church
  Formation, 116–127; General Conference, 129, 130; General Superintendent, 131; General Sec-

retary-treasurer, 133; General Board, 133; Executive Board, 134; manner of election, 135, 136; voting constituency, 136; district organization, 137–139; local churches, 140; ministerial membership, 140; doctrinal position, 141, 142; stand against error, 143–146; headquarters, 146–150; publications, 150–156; foreign missions, 156 to 159; home missions, 159–162; youth, 162–165; Sunday school, 165–168; Ladies Auxiliary, 168 to 170; Editorial Department, 170 to 172; Pentecostal Publishing House, 172, 173; printing division, 173, 174; Harvestime, 174–176; Department of Education, 176 to 178; endorsed Bible schools, 178, 179; Tupelo Children's Mansion, 180–182; organizational growth, 182

Urshan, Andrew D., 14, 18, 32, 41, 54, 190, 191
Urshan, Nathaniel A., 176

Vouga, Oscar, 95, 100, 119, 121, 133, 158, 195, 196

Wallace, J. O., 155, 166, 173
Weidner, J. Roy, 166
Western Apostolic Bible College, 179, 180
Whittington, W. H., 36, 60, 64, 65
Wolff, M. J., 154

Yadon, C. Haskell, 160, 176
Youth
  Organization, 46, 78, 79, 97, 98, 162, 163; names, 46, 56, 97, 162; officials, 46, 79, 97, 162, 163; Sheaves for Christ, 163, 164; periodical (Conquerors Tread), 164; other activities, 164, 165